THE END OF KARMA

Also by Dharma Singh Khalsa, M.D.

Books

Brain Longevity (Warner Books, 1997)

The Pain Cure (Warner Books, 1999)

Meditation as Medicine
(Pocket Books—Simon & Schuster, 2001)

Food as Medicine
(Atria Books—Simon & Schuster, 2003)

The New Golden Rules (Hay House, 2005)

Kit

The Better Memory Kit (Hay House, 2004)

CDs

(A series of 7 CDs with Spirit Voyage Music)
First Chakra: Morning Call
Second Chakra Meditation
Meditations for the Third and Fifth Chakras
Fourth Chakra: Meditation for a Calm Heart
Sixth Chakra Meditation
Seventh and Eighth Chakras:
Meditation to Heal Self and Others
Wake Up to Wellness

Love Is In You, by Dr. Khalsa's group, Bliss,
featuring Dr. D and Master L
(presents a unique combination of pop/
rock melodies and inspiring words.
Created to uplift and enlighten © 2004 drdharma Music)

Audiocassette

Meditation for Healing:
A Dialogue Between Dharma Singh Khalsa, M.D.,
and Deepak Chopra, M.D. (Hay House, 2003)

Please visit Hay House USA: **www.hayhouse.com;**
Hay House Australia: **www.hayhouse.com.au;**
Hay House UK: **www.hayhouse.co.uk;**
Hay House South Africa: **orders@psdprom.co.za**

THE END OF
KARMA

40 Days to Perfect Peace, Tranquility, and Joy

Dharma Singh Khalsa, M.D.

HAY HOUSE, INC.
Carlsbad, California
London • Sydney • Johannesburg
Vancouver • Hong Kong

Copyright © 2005 by Dharma Singh Khalsa

Published and distributed in the United States by: Hay House, Inc., P.O. Box 5100, Carlsbad, CA 92018-5100 • *Phone:* (760) 431-7695 or (800) 654-5126 • *Fax:* (760) 431-6948 or (800) 650-5115 • www.hayhouse.com • *Published and distributed in Australia by:* Hay House Australia Pty. Ltd., 18/36 Ralph St., Alexandria NSW 2015 • *Phone:* 612-9669-4299 • *Fax:* 612-9669-4144 • www.hayhouse.com.au • *Published and distributed in the United Kingdom by:* Hay House UK, Ltd. • Unit 62, Canalot Studios • 222 Kensal Rd., London W10 5BN • *Phone:* 44-20-8962-1230 • *Fax:* 44-20-8962-1239 • www.hayhouse.co.uk • *Published and distributed in the Republic of South Africa by:* Hay House SA (Pty), Ltd., P.O. Box 990, Witkoppen 2068 • *Phone/Fax:* 27-11-706-6612 • orders@psdprom.co.za • *Distributed in Canada by:* Raincoast • 9050 Shaughnessy St., Vancouver, B.C. V6P 6E5 • *Phone:* (604) 323-7100 • *Fax:* (604) 323-2600

Editorial supervision: Jill Kramer • *Design:* Julie Davison

Library of Congress Cataloging-in-Publication Data

Singh Khalsa, Dharma.
  The end of karma : 40 days to perfect peace, tranquility, and joy / Dharma Singh Khalsa.
    p. cm.
  ISBN-13: 978-1-4019-0641-2 (hardcover)
  ISBN-10: 1-4019-0641-9 (hardcover)
  1. Spiritual life. I. Title.

BL624.S567 2005
294.5'44--dc22

2005015182

ISBN 13: 978-1-4019-0641-2
ISBN 10: 1-4019-0641-9

08   07   06   05   4 3 2 1
1st printing, September 2005

Printed in the United States of America

This book is dedicated to you.
As you read it, you will be
transformed, and know the
unknown mystery within yourself. . . .

Contents

PART II: TWO MEDITATIONS TO END YOUR KARMA

INTRODUCTION

The Purpose of Life

God is only one, the doer of everything . . . this is also your true identity.

This book will help you realize the true identity of your own personal Divinity.

The Age of Mindless Suffering Is Over

Thank you for joining me in this time and space, where you've been drawn by your destiny to take the next step in your spiritual growth. We're now entering the Age of Aquarius, where our spiritual identity shall be our reason for living. Only then will we be able to create peace on Earth during our lifetime and leave the world better for those who come after us.

Love is the motivating force to experience our higher consciousness. It has many stages, the highest of which is love for the self. Yet the master stage is only found in the love of the highest being, or the self within the self. The words in this book are directed toward, and touch, that deepest part of your being, your soul. When you take care of yourself in this way—that is, by touching your soul and activating your spirit—many wonderful benefits ensue, including better health, greater happiness, and enhanced peace of mind.

Think of a tiny little acorn. Now imagine holding it in your hand. . . . It's beautiful and complete in itself, isn't it? But where is the oak tree? If you take a few moments to think about it, perhaps you'll realize that the oak tree is inside the acorn. How can that be? Well, while in the ground, that little acorn will attract to it everything it needs to become a mighty oak tree: It will have all the sun, water, rain, minerals from the soil, and blessings of the Creator to grow into that tree.

You don't even have to dig it up and inspect it—the complete transformation of the acorn into a grand oak tree is going to happen elegantly as part of the natural flow of life. So, too, can you be transformed into the beautiful oak tree of your own spirit by getting in the flow of this book. All you have to do is follow the path I'll describe in a moment and let nature take its course.

I am a medical doctor who was originally trained as an anesthesiologist. In 1981 I met the man I recognized as my spiritual teacher, Yogi Bhajan. After meeting him, I realized that I no longer had to use powerful anesthetic drugs to put people to sleep; rather, I now understood that I could use alternative forms of healing (such as yoga, meditation, and nutrition) to help individuals wake up and heal in their body, mind, and soul. And so, I decided that I wanted to devote my life to helping people live healthier, happier, and more successful lives. I have done just that, being considered by many to be a leading pioneer in the field of integrative medicine (my specialty is helping people prevent and reverse memory loss). I've even been invited to testify before Congress about my ideas for building a better memory, and later met with the surgeon general, who supported my work.

Because I wanted to totally immerse myself in the same lifestyle practiced by my teacher, I decided to also become a Sikh. In case you're new to my work or aren't familiar with Sikhs, let me take a moment here to explain. Sikhism is a lifestyle religion that originated in India. The Sikh faith has little dogma and a lot of soul—Sikhs simply believe in One God and in helping people, regardless of their religion or station in life. My wife (who is from Rome, Italy) and I, along with many Westerners, converted to Sikhism because of our relationship with Yogi Bhajan.

Yogi Bhajan, who passed from his physical body to his heavenly abode in October 2004, came to America in 1969 and began training teachers. Many of his students wanted to totally embrace his way of life, as I did, so they also chose to become Sikhs, in addition to being his yoga students. That's one reason why you'll see many people wearing white turbans and teaching kundalini yoga and meditation as taught by Yogi Bhajan at so many conferences on health and healing across the United States and around the world.

What Is Karma, and How Can You Possibly End it?

Many people think of karma as something concerning a leftover debt from a past life. But karma, in my view, has absolutely nothing to do with either past lives or future incarnations. It's what's happening right now. As best-selling author Deepak Chopra writes in *The Seven Spiritual Laws of Success:*

> Every action generates a force of energy
> that returns to us in like kind . . .
> what we sow is what we reap.
>
> And when we choose actions that bring
> happiness and success to others,
> the fruit of our karma is happiness and success.

Deepak then goes on to say, "'Karma' is both action and the consequence of that action; it is cause and effect simultaneously, because every action generates a force of energy that returns to us in like kind."

As you read *this* book, you'll notice that your focus, attraction, and intention will begin to shift toward your Higher Power, or the God within yourself. Therefore, that's what will return to you—you will tune in to the God within you. By reading this book, you'll be drawn to your Higher Power and your best self. As you'll see in a moment, that's not karma—it's what I call "dharma."

As a doctor and an ordained minister, I've consulted with many people who were so stuck in their lives that they were miserable. Their actions and behaviors had created the same negative results over and over again—time after time, they felt confined in a bad relationship, let's say, never seeming to learn from their past mistakes. Others stayed in the same dead-end job, even though they knew that there was something better for them elsewhere. Additional patients of mine lived with the same mental or physical pain for years.

One was a middle-aged woman who'd had multiple difficult relationships with men . . . as you might guess, she'd also had an abusive relationship with her father. From a psychological point of view, this woman was continually trying to re-create that original relationship with her father with the men she dated. Why? Because to her this symbolized love—it was all she knew. That's karma.

When my client finally had the realization that she could move beyond that destructive type of relationship, she experienced a quantum leap forward in her happiness level and enjoyment of life. That's dharma in action.

What Is Dharma?

As Deepak Chopra pointed out, karma is essentially about cause and effect. While it's true that there will always be cause and effect, the difference between karma and dharma is that when you live your dharma, you end your karma. Dharma eats up karma simply because dharma is a higher plane of existence. It's spiritual living in action.

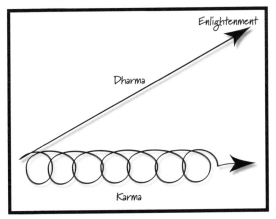

Living your dharma, which transcends karma, is when you live each day in touch with your highest or best self. This is your spirit. The more you live dharma and spirit, the more you stop going 'round and 'round, creating karma for yourself. This helps you maintain balance and stability in your life—and that's what this book is about.

We all have many sides to our personalities, from the shadow to the light. While it may be somewhat fashionable, philosophically interesting, or psychologically important to know all sides of yourself, I'm not one to say, "Embrace your dark side. Embrace your shadow."

In contrast, I say, "Manifest your light until your shadow disappears." That's dharma.

How do you increase your light? Don't worry, this book will share a very simple way with you. But first, perhaps the following story will help deepen your understanding of dharma.

The Man

One day my wife and I were in San Francisco on a speaking tour. We were having lunch downtown in a small café when we both noticed a very saintly looking older man walk by. He wore a turban and had a long white beard, and we immediately knew two things: He was from India, and he was a Sikh (as we are).

So this older gentleman came up to us, and we began to chat. He asked me my name, and I told him what it was. "Oh," he replied, "Dharma is a very important name."

From the moment I first saw it written down on a piece of tan paper in Yogi Bhajan's own handwriting, I've always loved my spiritual name, which I received on Thanksgiving weekend in 1981. Yet up until now, I'd thought that it meant "a pure lion on a victorious path."

Now, the man looked at me very deeply and said, "Dharma is that one who always remembers God." Then, after a few more moments, he walked out of the restaurant.

When I told my spiritual brother, Livtar Singh, about this event, he simply stated, "You created him to remind you of who you are."

I answered, "You mean God sent him?"

"We're all God," was his reply.

That type of thinking is the epitome of dharma.

Livtar's comments produced an "aha" moment for me, a time of great understanding. I'm very grateful to the Universe for bringing forth that happening in my life because it helped me become very clear about this book that you're holding in your hands. I realized that by reading it, you'll find that your ultimate destiny is to always remember God, too. Beyond that, there is nothing!

I know how important your family is to you, and I know how much you want to find the right work to do. But believe me, your highest destiny as a spiritual woman or man has nothing to do with that. Your ultimate destiny, just like mine, is to always remember God.

Astoundingly, new medical research reveals how true this actually is. It seems that scientists have asked the following two questions: (1) "Is God in our genes?" and (2) "Does our DNA compel us to seek a Higher Power?"

Believe it or not, the answer to both questions is "Yes!"

The results of this research reveal that we all have a God gene, which, when activated, allows us to have the kind of experiences called "transcendence," "bliss," or "ecstasy." This spiritual gene establishes a feeling of rapture within us. In other words, it's possible to have the experience of feeling God. Moreover, according to science, it's desirable for your long-term well-being to have the experience of shaking hands with God often. Science tells us that being in touch with your spirit, your Higher Power, or the God within will help you become healthier and happier, and it can even lengthen your lifespan. *The End of Karma* is designed to help you have that experience of feeling God within your being every day of your life.

How This Book Works

As a spiritual seeker, you're no doubt aware of the importance of positive self-talk. And if you meditate, you almost certainly know the powerful effects that a mantra can have. Moreover, as a person who has perhaps read books by Louise Hay, the founder of Hay House (the publisher of this book), you also know about the incredible healing power of affirmations. As I'm sure you've discovered, affirmations can change you for the better at a very deep level of your being.

The words, meditations, and spiritual thoughts that make up this book are very effective affirmations, for they speak directly to your highest self. They penetrate your spiritual essence, thus taking you to the next stage of your personal growth—toward experiencing your Higher Power on a daily basis. This is important because I believe that the whole issue of spirituality has become way too complicated. It's been made far too philosophical and intellectual, when in reality, spirituality is actually quite easy to understand.

God is within you; and you have the right to experience that peace, happiness, and joy while living on Earth in the here-and-now, regardless of your circumstances in life. *The End of Karma* will help you awaken to that truth within you.

Practical and beyond intellectualization, this little book will transport you effortlessly into the realm of spirit and soul. Reading, meditating upon, and studying each of these chapters in succession, preferably first thing in the morning, will help you move from traveling on the too-often bumpy highway of fate to the smooth royal road toward your destiny: that of being a very loving person living a highly spiritual life.

The words in the body of this book were originally written by a great master named Guru Nanak more than 500 years ago. He called this work *Japji Sahib,* or "respected meditation of the soul." These words have the power to speak directly to your soul.

Here is how the original words came to pass. One day, Nanak, as he was known before becoming a guru, went for his morning bath in a river near his home in northern India. He entered the water and was not seen again for three days. His family feared that he'd drowned. Then he reappeared and began singing the very verses you'll find within these pages. Nanak said that as he entered the water, God spoke to him, giving him this discourse. Thereafter, he became known as Guru Nanak.

Guru Nanak, along with his musician companion, Mardana, traveled far and wide in the late 15th and early 16th centuries through what are now northern India, Pakistan, Tibet, Iran, and southeast Asia. Guru Nanak always traveled on foot, and he brought together people of different religions and social classes to sit together in love. They sang meditative songs of the Creator and the greatness of life.

Guru Nanak was a pioneer and a revolutionary, tearing down the walls of prejudice against women in Asia 500 years ago. He saw the Divine Light of the Creator in men and women equally, and established a path where women were held in the highest honor. For that, his legacy lives on in the hearts and souls of millions of people around the world.

I feel deeply in my heart that it's time to share Guru Nanak's wonderful and lovely words with you, which is why I've chosen to write this book. The translation of Guru Nanak's beautiful words has been brought forth by a young woman named Ek Ong Kaar Kaur Khalsa, from her book, *Japji Sahib: The Song of the Soul*. They are used with her kind cooperation.

At the outset of each chapter you will find a short sentence depicting the benefits of that particular section as described by Yogi Bhajan. After the poetic verse, I will render my interpretation of it, and suggest a follow-up idea for you to enhance your daily experience. Finally, there's a space at the end of each chapter in which I invite you to record your own thoughts and ideas on that particular section. I promise that you'll find that action very enlightening.

I'd like to point out that you may occasionally find the book repetitious . . . but that's a good thing. It acts like a mantra, which, as you're probably aware, is repeated over and over again, often linked to a particular breathing pattern. The words of these chapters act like many beautiful mantras: They have a beneficial effect that, as mentioned above, I describe at the beginning of each one. Moreover, as you'll soon see, several of the chapters are similar or in the same vein—this is done because certain points need emphasis. As the book progresses, the ideas and thoughts conveyed by its words will lead you to a very high level of spiritual experience.

The best way to use this book is to read and reflect upon one chapter a day for 40 days. The best time to read the book is when you first wake up in the morning. The world is still and quiet early in the morning, and the static of life has yet to interfere with your ability to touch your soul. If you wait too long or start too late in the day, you may feel harried, rushed, or frenetic, and that's not conducive to meditating on the words of this book. So start your day in a positive way—begin another glorious morning by touching your soul and activating your higher spiritual power. Shaking hands with God every morning is the best way to reap the benefits found in this work.

The 40 chapters herein are followed by a very special meditation section, which contains two mind/body exercises for you to practice. They both help end your karma—the first brings harmony to your life by stimulating your life force and balancing your five elements (earth, air, water, wood, and fire); the second has the very beneficial effect of uniting the unending circle of infinite prosperity. You can choose to practice one or both of them after reading and reflecting upon your chapter of the day. If you do want to meditate using one of the exercises in Part II, you'll have to go to that section after reading your Chapter of the day. Then you'll probably want to recheck the instructions almost every time you meditate until you know them well. Alternatively, you can wait until you've read all 40 chapters to begin doing the meditations. You'll enjoy them whenever you choose; they're like icing on the cake.

At the end of 40 days, your karma will end, and you'll be in touch with your dharma.

Living Your Dharma

Living your dharma is at first about making choices, such as serving others and meditating regularly. As your unconscious mind is cleansed, however, God comes to sit in your heart, and the ending of your karma begins. Karma then shifts to dharma, and karma is complete. Your soul is now fully awakened. Reading this book will take years, perhaps lifetimes, off that process.

It is said by many of today's writers of spiritual books that everyone has a unique purpose in life, perhaps a special talent or gift that will help them serve others and live to their highest potential. That is in part true. But reaching your true highest goal in life—that is, the realization of your Divine spiritual nature and being able to see God in all—may have nothing whatsoever to do with your vocation. Recall that dharma means always trying to remember God in all you do throughout the busy hours of the day. That's your real work and the purpose of life.

This concept is summed up best in the writings of a wonderful man who also lived in India many hundreds of years ago. His name is Guru Arjan Dev. As we're all getting older, I'm sure you'll probably relate to Arjan's very simple and poetic words:

Life is shortening day and night
Oh, my mind, meet the Guru Inside
(The Divine Guide)
And set yourself right.

The world in which we find ourselves living today, it seems to me, is engrossed in intensity, anxiety, and greater stress then ever before. As you end your karma by living in the lap of your highest and best self every day, I guarantee that you'll find it easier and more joyous to be in this world.

Study and meditate upon the words contained on these pages. By doing so, you'll gain the true commodity for which you've been born—that is, realizing your Divine inner being. Then you'll have a greater experiential awareness of the God that resides inside of you. You'll be happy and at peace, and then you'll be able to help create peace in the world. That will, once and for all, fulfill all of your dreams and heart's desires.

So off you go on the voyage of a lifetime, perhaps your most important one yet. Prepare yourself for a journey to the center of your soul (and do remember to center yourself and breathe deeply before and after every chapter).

My love and blessings are with you.

PART I

The Song of the Soul

CHAPTER 1

We Are One with God

*Meditating on this chapter removes fate
and changes destiny to prosperity.*

One Spirit Beyond
Moves within the Creation—
Coordinating
Consolidating
Continually
Creating,

And this Spirit
Within me
Is my True Identity.

It Does All
And Causes All
To be Done.

It Protects me
Through all incidents
Of Time and Space.

It fears nothing
And knows nothing
Of vengeance
Or anger.

Deathless
It comes into Form.

In Itself, It has
Never been born.

Flowing through the cycles
Of Birth and Death,
It moves
By Its Own
Purity and Projection.

This understanding
Shall come to you
As a sweet blessing,
As a gift.

In every moment
Continue
In Its Continual
Remembrance.

From the start
This Truth was True.

All through Time and Space
Is True.

Even now,
This Truth is True.

Nanak, this ever shall be True.

Understanding This Chapter

God is All and Everything—this is the greatest truth there is and shall ever be. If you can make this thought your own and live it, your karma is complete. Your job is done when you know that your Creator, His creation, and you are one and the same. By reflecting on and understanding this chapter, you shall come to understand all of spirituality and easily feel God close at hand.

When you digest this chapter, you'll be well on your way to leading a life of peace, tranquility, and joy. You'll have no problems as you come to realize that all things come from God and all things go back to God. This is a natural fact, a basic law of spirituality.

If you don't understand that God is everything by the time you're finished reading this book, you will. As my own spiritual master, Yogi Bhajan, always said: "If you can't see God in all, you can't see God at all."

Please let go of your ingrained notion of sin. You are perfect, created in the image of God. If He could have created anything better, He would have . . . but He didn't. You are you and you are God and you are perfect. So be like God: Be loving, courageous, and forgiving to yourself and everyone else. Try it, and see how great you are.

Everything in existence may come and go, but God is everlasting. So is your soul, because God and you are one and the same. You are a living example of life everlasting, and your soul shall never die. God is an all-pervading energy and a glorious light. It's your true mission in life, your dharma, to let your spirit shine and your soul glow.

Everything you've just read is entirely possible; when it happens, no matter how quickly or how long it takes, it is by His Grace. It doesn't belong to you; it is God. When you find this power within yourself, you come to know your innermost soul, and it is by His grace.

But in the meantime, you must do the work.

Putting This Chapter to Work in Your Life

Affirm: *As I come to feel that God is all there really is, I witness how my life becomes more peaceful and relaxed. I come to understand that true prosperity is living life in balance, free from the anxieties that may arise from the ups and downs of life's changes.*

My Reflections on This Chapter

_____

_____

_____

_____

_____

_____

_____

_____

CHAPTER 2

By Thinking, Nothing Happens

*Feeling this chapter deeply gives knowledge and
ecstasy of God. It is an antidote to depression.*

You think and think
Ten-thousand thoughts,
But not one thought
Will give you
What you seek.

You sit in silence
To find the silence
But silence never comes.
Your spirit always sings
The song of the Divine.

And all your troubles,
And all your cares,

These will never fade away
Though you may hoard
Every treasure in the world.

And all the clever tricks
You use,
The countless little tricks—
Not even one
Will go along with you.

How can we find
The House of Truth?

How can we break
This wall of lies?

Surrender yourself
And walk the Way
Of Spirit's Will.
Oh my soul,
Be with what
Is already written.

Understanding This Chapter

This delightful chapter is of profound significance. In it, the existential predicament of the human being is explained, and an answer is given. Philosophizing, silent meditation, lots of money, and intellectual subtleties are of little or no use in effacing the false self and realizing the true one.

How can this mask that so many people hide behind be dissolved, and how can we attain the true self? There is only one way: The veil of illusion can be opened by surrendering our will to God's Will. It is the Will of our Highest Being that governs the Universe and its laws.

God's Will for you, or your ultimate truth—the realization of which is the purpose of your birth—is written in your soul. Your destiny is not to be a doctor or a writer or a social worker. Your destiny is to uncover your Divinity, which resides inside of you.

The Absolute Reality is spiritual and can't be grasped by the mind. Therefore, thinking about it does not (unfortunately) bring you one step closer to its realization. Neither does philosophizing. It is only by the dissolution of your sense of the "I, me, mine" philosophy that your ego gets out of the way and you discover your true identity, which gives you a glimpse of your soul's path.

Ego, however, is a deep-rooted disease, because under its influence human beings have a tendency to become individualized and separate from the wholeness of the Universe and each other. We devise boundaries, creating an "us versus them" mentality. We don't recognize that we are all one. We see people as different: different colors, different countries, different religions. Over eons, this particular mind-set hasn't changed, and it's led to war and more war.

You have to move beyond the veil of the superficial mind, which is engrossed in ego, to elevate it to a higher region, that of truth. The limitless soul is restricted by ego, and its outlook becomes narrow. You then can't see reality clearly because a barrier is created between you and God. Consequently, light is shut out, and you wander from one error or misdeed to another. The result is that you have to be reborn and perhaps reborn again—not necessarily in another life, but in this one until you get on the right track. This process of wandering around, repeating the same mistakes over and over again, is called "transmigration," and it's the root cause of much of the unhappiness and violence seen in the world today. This is karma at its worst.

Under the influence of the ego, people find joy and pleasure in trivialities, shadows, and the artificial stimulation of an adrenaline rush. One must return to a higher energy, attuned to His Will, in order to escape this trap. When the personal equation has disappeared, the will is recognized.

Where did the ego come from in the first place? If you said, "His Will," then you're starting to catch on to the game. The idea is to face the ego, which was given by His Will, and work through the karma of yesterday to emerge in the golden light of the dharma of tomorrow.

The will of God is essentially His order for you. If God is all, and God is in you, His Will then becomes *your* will when you live in a certain manner. When your actions are correctly in tune with the Divine, your free will and God's order are one and the same. Similarly, when you're not tuned in, instead of enjoying peace, tranquility, and bliss, you experience pain, misery, and conflict.

Some seekers try to realize their Higher Power by remaining silent, but few reach such a depth of that state where they can discover the true self behind the mask. You can keep trying, but know that your progress will be imperceptible. As a Westerner, you don't have the time to stay on retreat 24/7 for enough years to get where you need to go. After all, you aren't a monk.

You can be incredibly wealthy, yet you won't feel satisfied unless you're also living a life connected to your soul. Many fabulously wealthy individuals are also the unhappiest, as they still feel the weight of the world on their back. Piling up loads of worldly goods won't bring you any closer to Him—you'll still have a great longing for the touch of your soul. In fact, at the end of your life, all of your cleverness will be meaningless because it won't have taken you any closer to the inner peace that we all desire.

So how can you move beyond this mask of illusion found in your ego? If you respond that the way is to discover, surrender, and live God's Will for you, then you're on the road to ending your karma.

The coming chapters discuss this notion further and eventually tell you how.

Putting This Chapter to Work in Your Life

Affirm: *Today I will begin the process of attuning my will to that of the will of the Divine.*

Next, inhale through your nose and say the sound "Sat" (rhymes with "but"); then exhale and say the sound "Nam" (rhymes with "Mom"). All breathing is through the nose. Repeat for one minute out loud, one minute in a whisper, one minute silently, one minute in a whisper, and one minute out loud.

Finish by taking a few long, slow, deep breaths in and out through your nose. Please hold the final breath in for a count of ten, then exhale and relax.

My Reflections on This Chapter

_____

_____

_____

_____

_____

_____

_____

When you live a life of spirit, one in which you're on a search for the sacred and tuned in to God's Will for you, your actions will then be high. This is living your dharma, and that is God's Will in action.

You're probably familiar with the sayings "As you sow, so shall you reap" or "What goes around comes around." Both of these are great examples of the cause and effect of karma . . . but they can also mean dharma if your actions are in tune with His Will.

A great sage once said, "The flowing pen of His Will runs according to your own deeds." As we shall soon see, you must look within yourself to hear the still, small voice of the Enlightener and receive Divine guidance.

Putting This Chapter to Work in Your Life

Affirm: *Today I will list some of the causes and effects in my own life. I will ask myself which are ego based or karma and which are dharma.*

My Reflections on This Chapter

_____

_____

_____

_____

_____

_____

_____

CHAPTER 4

Someone Is Singing

Understanding this chapter turns insufficiency into sufficiency, depression into elevation, and low self-esteem into high self-confidence.

When the soul
Tunes in
To the Infinite

And spontaneously sings
With Divine love and joy,

In that soul-singing,
Some capture Your power.

But who has the power
To capture Your power?

When the soul
Tunes in
To the Infinite

And spontaneously sings
With Divine love and joy,

In that soul-singing
Some sing of You
As a Giver
And know giving
As the sign of You.

When the soul
Tunes in
To the Infinite

And spontaneously sings
With Divine love and joy,

In that soul-singing
Some sing of
Your virtues,
The elements You use
To create life,
And how amazing
It all is.
How magnificently beautiful.

When the soul
Tunes in
To the Infinite

And spontaneously sings
With Divine love and joy,

In that soul-singing
Some sing
Of the knowledge
That can only be gotten
By arduous study.

When the soul
Tunes in
To the Infinite

And spontaneously sings
With Divine love and joy,

In that soul-singing
Some sing
Of the Power that
Creates all things
Sustains them
And destroys them.

When the soul
Tunes in
To the Infinite

And spontaneously sings
With Divine love and joy,

In that soul-singing
Some sing
Of how You
Take the souls away
And then
Give them back again.

When the soul
Tunes in
To the Infinite,

And spontaneously sings
With Divine love and joy

In that soul-singing,
Some sing
Of how far beyond
Our reach, our grasp
You are.

When the soul
Tunes in
To the Infinite

And spontaneously sings
With Divine love and joy,

In that soul-singing
Some sing
You are always with us.

There is no end
To what
We can say
About You.

Millions of people
Speak
Millions of ways.

You, Great Giver,
Keep giving to us
And we grow tired
Of just taking.

Age after age
You continually
Feed and
Nourish us.

In Your Will,
Oh Divine Spirit,
You guide us along
The path You choose for us.
The Seeker of Spirit,
Blissful,
Hasn't a care.

Understanding This Chapter

There are many, many people who by education or title consider themselves experts on God and His ways. The reality is, however, that we can only speak of and glorify Him according to our own limited human knowledge and experience. None of us, therefore, can fully express all of the excellences inherent in the Creator or the creation. None of us can know God completely unless we're as high as He is, yet no human being can ever be that high.

We human beings are so often out of touch with the fact that God, or our Higher Power, or the Creator has given us so many blessings that we've forgotten them. Yet we keep on receiving, praying for more, and taking what we can get, without taking the time to remember that it all comes from His Will and is a gift. We forget that every single breath of life we have is a gift from our Creator, and when the breath stops, life as we know it here on Earth is done.

What I'd be pleased to have you note, though, is that when you do begin to remember your Higher Self, you'll live happy and carefree. You are then joyous and in bliss.

Yes, it's true that the amount we understand is directly related to our experience, but we can all develop that higher knowledge and experience—we just have to work at it. Some have written that the word *jap* means to meditate on God's name, which it certainly does—there's no argument about that. But the actual meaning of the word *jap* is to repeat, and repeat, and repeat some more. That is what begins the process of tuning in to the will of the Divine, which resides in your heart.

We'll consider that in the next chapter.

Putting This Chapter to Work in Your Life

Affirm: *Today I will be grateful for every breath of life that I am most fortunate to receive. I will try to live in that consciousness as often as I can during the busy hours of my day. When the static of my life stops for a moment and I find some space, I will again return to my breath and feel eternally grateful.*

My Reflections on This Chapter

_____

_____

_____

_____

_____

_____

_____

✤ ✤ ✤

CHAPTER 5

Covering Your Karmas

*Meditating on this chapter helps you break
through the trap of feeling poor or without means.*

True is the Master
Of Creation.

True is His Spirit
Within me.

Speak it with Infinite Love.

We call on You
And beg to You,
"Give me, give me."

And you, Great Giver,
Give it All.

What can we
Place before You
That will allow us
To see the splendor
Of Your Divine and Noble Court?

What words can we speak
With our own lips
That, upon hearing,
You would touch us
With Your Love?

In the Amrit Veyla,
The still hours before sunrise,
Our True Spirit
Becomes known
As we meditate upon
Your Greatness.

By the consequences
Of our positive past actions,
We have been gifted
This robe of human form.

Grace leads us
To the gate of liberation
Found within it.
Oh Seeker of Spirit
In this way know,
All people
Hold the Truth
Within themselves.

Understanding This Chapter

Now that you've seen what doesn't work when it comes to knowing your Higher Power, I'd like to explore what *does*.

Why is it important to make this connection in the first place? Because your true nature is that of spirit, and if you don't get in touch with it, genuine happiness and satisfaction will be difficult to attain. Moreover, true prosperity in your life and the fulfillment of your dreams are virtually impossible without developing and sustaining a bond with your soul. The reality is that where you place your intention, attention, and energy is what you will manifest. So, to realize the God within requires you to place your focus on doing just that.

God, the Giver, gives and gives so much that most people take all their bounties for granted. So the question arises: What can you, as a human being who's looking for that special relationship with Him, do to make progress toward that goal?

The answer is very clear: "Get up with the sun, put your attention on God, and concentrate on Him."

The ambrosial hours are the sweet, quiet, and still moments in the early morning before dawn when the sun is at about a 30-degree angle with the earth. This angle has a profoundly positive effect on the magnetic field of our planet and, therefore, on your energy as well. When you get up later, it's difficult to carve out the time to become one with the One. You're in too much of a hurry to begin your day, to get to work, and so on. This connection isn't something you just want to squeeze in, or your whole spiritual life will be tight, constricted, and devoid of significant meaning.

As I mentioned briefly in the Introduction (and will discuss in greater detail in Part II of this book), modern medical research confirms the wisdom of the ancients. Using sophisticated x-rays, such as various types of brain scans, scientists have discovered that when you meditate you change the anatomical picture of your brain. After a certain period of time, ranging from 12 minutes to one hour (depending on the type of meditation or prayer used [Kundalini meditation for the former, and Buddhist and rosary for the latter]), people's brains show a rise in their frontal-lobe activity. This signifies increased attention.

At the same time, a drop in the activity in a different area of the brain, which has become known as "The God Spot," occurs. Additionally, two other extraordinary events take place: (1) People report being in touch with their Higher Power; and (2) their brain chemicals, which are also measured in the research, show a picture of happiness. The same chemicals that go down in depression, for example, go up here.

Isn't it fascinating to learn that happiness is directly correlated with a spiritual event? In fact, that's exactly what the people studied report: They feel happy. Other studies at Harvard Medical School, for example, have shown that when you do meditate on a regular basis, you feel the presence of a Higher Being with you all the time. Along with that, further research reveals that regular meditators are healthier and live longer.

It's our true nature, our essence (or the *Nam*, as the ancients call it), to be spiritual. It's also our true nature to be peaceful and happy . . . that's bliss, or heaven on Earth. So, you see, you don't have to die to get to heaven—you can enjoy the kingdom of heaven in the here-and-now. But, again, you have to do some work. It's simply a natural law.

When you meditate on the Nam, or your true nature, in the ambrosial hours of the morning, you become a much deeper person, aware of all the subtler workings of the Universe. When you open up your consciousness, great things begin to happen. As you become one with God, you begin to develop many wonderful attributes associated with God: love, patience, forgiveness, tolerance, tranquility, and inner peace. Then anything is possible.

Moreover, as enough of us develop higher consciousness, and we develop a critical mass, the world will change automatically because we're all linked. Our connection is through what's called "a powerful unified field." In other words, my thoughts may be able to create peace in the world by themselves, but when they're combined with your thoughts (and everyone else's thoughts that are of a like-minded nature), the potential for positive change on Earth multiplies significantly.

When you finally understand that we are all one, that's how you're able to end karma and move up to living a life of dharma or right action, and higher values in the now.

Putting This Chapter to Work in Your Life

Affirm: *Today I will start my day in a positive way. I will create some extra time to meditate during the ambrosial hours of the dawn.* (See Part II for suggested meditations.)

My Reflections on This Chapter

_____

_____

_____

_____

_____

_____

_____

_____

CHAPTER 6

May I Never Forget Him

*Mastering this chapter grants success when
you have a sense of failure within yourself
and don't feel up to a job.*

Nothing has
Established You
Or placed You
On Your throne.

Neither are You
Created by anything.

You within Yourself
Are pure
Like the crystal
Cool, clear water
Of a stream.

Those who serve You,
You bestow upon them
So much honor.

I sing
Of Your virtues,
Your priceless gifts and treasures.

Sing.
Deeply listen.
And oh my mind
Overflow with Love.

All suffering shall vanish,
And peace,
Sweet peace,
Shall make its home
In your heart.

The wise person
Who flows
With the integrity
Of the Teacher's words
Is one
With the Naad,
The subtle vibration
Which powers creation.

The wise person
Who flows
With the integrity

Of the Teacher's words
Is one
With all scriptures written
And yet to be written.

The wise person
Who flows
With the integrity
Of the Teacher's words
Remains continually
Within herself
With Thee.

The Guru,
The Divine Teacher,
Can take the form
Of Shiva.

That Guru
Can take the form
Of Vishnu or Brahma.

That Divine Teacher
Can even take the form
Of the Divine Mother.

Even if I know all this,
Still there's no way
To speak it,
No matter how much I say.

The Divine Teacher
Has given me
One lesson to learn.

All souls come
From the hand of One Giver.

May I never, ever
Forget Him.

Understanding This Chapter

Your highest state of being can't be established by anyone and is beyond time, space, and description. Your best self is everywhere and exists always—so the idea is not to just ritually meditate, but rather to inscribe that energy within yourself.

Everything comes from your daily spiritual practice. Once you incorporate this habit into your life, then suffering, obstruction, conflict, and unhappiness leave you. Thereafter, pure joy and elevated consciousness come to live in your heart. Through meditation on your Divine essence (or what many advanced spiritualists call the "Nam" or "Sat Nam"), spiritual knowledge can effortlessly come into your mind. Ultimately, your goal is to come to dwell in that space where with your every breath you are in tune with that energy.

We've come into this human form to discover our true self, which is the spark of the Divine that resides within us. After you have the realization that God lives within you, you live in bliss because you're always in touch with your spiritual self. Always remember that we are spiritual beings enjoying a human birth—we aren't humans somehow searching for spirit. You may have that thought, but it's an illusion. You are already everything you need to be; you simply have to continue to find that self within the self. When you discover your Divinity, you'll be able to more closely align yourself with your true purpose in life, finding the God within. Thereafter, you'll discover tremendous satisfaction through serving humanity with your greatest gifts and talents.

What's the greatest motivating force to experiencing your higher consciousness? The answer is love. Your spiritual development, or what we call "higher consciousness," has many stages of evolution. As I wrote in the Introduction, the highest stage of this evolution is love for the true self, the inner being. And the master stage of love is that of the highest being, which is within you right now.

Putting This Chapter to Work in Your Life

Affirm: *Today I will make an effort to lovingly cultivate my higher self by focusing my attention on my Higher Power, my immortal essence of reality, at various times throughout the busy hours of the day.*

My Reflections on This Chapter

_____

_____

_____

_____

_____

_____

_____

CHAPTER 7

Pleasing God

This chapter dispels limitations, traps, or coercion.

I wash myself
In sacred waters
In order to please You.

But if it doesn't please You,
What is the bathing for?

I see
The vastness of Your wondrous creation.

But without taking action,
How can I merge with Thee?

Within my own
Awareness

Are jewels, gems,
And rubies,
From listening to the teachings
Of the Divine Teacher
Even once.

All souls come
From the Hand of One Giver.

May I never, ever
Forget Him.

Understanding This Chapter

Although short and simple, this chapter crystallizes a number of very important concepts:

1. There's no substitute for doing the right thing according to your understanding of God's Will.

2. Experience, not talk or philosophy, is what you need to get to the next level in your spiritual growth.

3. There is no shortcut to enlightenment—you have to do the work.

4. If you work hard to understand these principles, you'll enjoy a new depth, richness, and wealth of beautiful spirit in your mind.

In this chapter, we're reminded that life is a great gift that shouldn't be wasted in trivial pursuits. The idea is to always keep the vibration and energy of your higher self in your thoughts, actions, and deeds, which will bring you great poise in dealing with the ups and downs of life.

So long as you employ your mind for fulfilling the lower desires of the body (such as anger, lust, greed, pride, or emotional attachment), you're a slave to your mind and not its master. Continuing on this lower path will keep you limited, without any idea of the unbounded power lying hidden within yourself.

This is made clear by the examples of saints and sages such as Jesus and Buddha, who broke the shackles of physical existence to prove that life is a living expression of the Divine music. So it is through the physical, manifest reality that your soul will evolve. Your mind creates problems that can be tamed only by your spirit—but life is real, to be lived and enjoyed.

This is our greatest hope, because nothing else has worked. Men, women, children, cities, and works of art have been exterminated wholesale by false religions based on nothing but ritual. Favoring living in the material world rather than focusing on spirit has created a society made up primarily of chaos, hate, and strife; and propagandists rule the day.

While it's true that poverty, disease, and hunger must be combatted on the physical plane, they're not the major causes of the problems in the world today. Unless the soul is enriched—and an overriding faith in spiritual values (such as service, practice, and love) gain superiority over temporal phenomena (such as an "us versus them" mentality) the world over—our future is bleak.

Our greatest hope for a bright future and a better world for our children and grandchildren is to develop a critical mass of spiritual seekers who value peace more than war, and love more than hate and intolerance. Why not begin today?

Putting This Chapter to Work in Your Life

Affirm: *Today I will begin to shift my thinking toward finding ways in which I can help create a circle of peace. Today I will try to keep peace in my heart, my mind, and my soul.*

My Reflections on This Chapter

_____

_____

_____

_____

_____

_____

_____

CHAPTER 8

Seeing the Unseen

Meditating on this chapter will heal you.

If a person were to live
Through the four ages
Or ten times that,

Known across
The nine continents
Followed by everyone.

Protected by a good name,
With fame and reputation
Received from the entire world.

Yet, if You do not look kindly
Our way, oh Divine One,

That position
Nobody would want.
Such a one would be
The worm
That lives inside worms.

Among criminals—
The most criminal.

Oh Seeker of Spirit,
The virtueless and the virtuous
Are both created by the Divine.

And what virtues they carry
Are given by Thee.

No one exists
Who can bestow virtues on You.

Understanding This Chapter

Here, not unlike a beautiful classical symphony, a theme is repeated. Again we learn about the futility and vanity of worrying about aging, or living a long life simply for its own sake. In neither is there any benefit to sovereign power, fame, and fortune; that is, unless God's gracious glance, which leads the soul to the One, is also there.

Beyond that, without any special spiritual blessing in your life, negative people will try to lay their guilt on you. With the mental strength and great energy given to you via spiritual living, you can resist the drag of those individuals who may live a lifestyle of lower thought and energy.

It's crucial for your spiritual growth to stay away from psychic vampires and live surrounded by like-minded people (those who support your spiritual life). In this way, your energy will rise and you will enjoy a life of exaltation.

Putting This Chapter to Work in Your Life

Affirm: *Today I will resolve to enjoy my life even more by being as carefree as possible, regardless of what is going on around me. This is blissful living.*

My Reflections on This Chapter

_____

_____

_____

_____

_____

_____

_____

CHAPTER 9

Listening

This chapter imparts the power to be a sage.

Those who are merged in You,
Those who spiritually lead,
Angels,
Masters
Deeply Listen.

The Earth,
And what holds the Earth,
And what surrounds the Earth
Inter-coordinate
By Deep Listening.

The Continents,
Other Realms,

Lower Worlds,
Work together
By Deep Listening.

Deeply Listening,
Death
Cannot touch you.

Oh my soul,
Those who surrender themselves in Love
To the Divine
Continually blossom and bloom.

Deeply Listening,
Sorrows
And errors
Depart.

Understanding This Chapter

Aha! Now we begin to go a little deeper. Here we learn that it's not enough to go through the phoniness of pretending to live a spiritual lifestyle. Nor is it sufficient to meditate every day in the early hours of the morning, although that is certainly an inviolate prerequisite to spiritual development. No, to go to the next level of your spiritual depth, you must begin to listen to the still, small voice within yourself. When you do, you'll realize that God's Will for you (which was discussed earlier) is right there inside of you, ready to be appreciated.

When you tune in and listen, your life changes. You no longer create such a big mess for yourself or someone else to clean up after. When you listen and follow the direction of your Higher Power, which you feel or hear, your chance of goofing up is much less. Then life becomes much more enjoyable, loving, and blissful. When you listen for God's Will within you, you begin to rise above physical consciousness and come into cosmic awareness. You are on your way to becoming a true spiritual person, and you begin to understand the mysteries of creation.

As the famous Sufi poet Kabir once commented, regarding the miraculous experience of hearing God's voice within your being: "When you transcend into the beyond, a subtle voice is heard. This voice only a person who is developing wisdom can hear."

This inner voice, heard in moments of concentrated meditation, is the true one of Divinely inspired wisdom. Your inner voice gives you direction toward the fulfillment of your highest destiny in this life. In that way, it takes you toward the immortal legacy of your soul.

Putting This Chapter to Work in Your Life

Affirm: *Today I will begin to learn to listen to the voice of my Higher Power within myself. I will create time during my meditation to just be, in the hopes of feeling the pulse of my own Divinity.*

My Reflections on This Chapter

_____

_____

_____

_____

_____

_____

_____

_____

❖ ❖ ❖

CHAPTER 10

Deeply Listening

Paying attention to this chapter expands your mind.

Deeply Listening,
The Three Aspects
Of the Divine—
Generator
Organizer
Deliverer/Destroyer—
Maintain their balance
And dance.

Deeply Listening,
Even those
With an imbalanced mind
Praise Thee
With their lips.

Deeply Listening,
Yoga
And the hidden systems
Of the body
Make themselves known.

Deeply Listening,
The wisdom
Of all sacred scriptures in the world
Is revealed.

Oh my soul,
Those who surrender themselves in Love
To the Divine
Continually blossom and bloom.

Deeply Listening,
Sorrows
And errors
Depart.

Understanding This Chapter

After you begin to listen to the voice within, the next step is to listen some more. Now you're probably noticing something that may be unexpected: Listening requires effort and commitment. You must be still and surrender yourself in a certain way that suspends your earthly desires, expectations, and attachments. You're now starting down the road to not simply knowing God, but to feeling His presence, too.

Listening is a transformational point in your life on the path toward the Divine. To hear the voice is a great act of love on both God's part and your own. It's a blossoming relationship, the seeds of which have been planted by reading, understanding, and meditating on all the previous chapters of this book.

This type of spiritual work has recently been studied from a scientific perspective, and the results are quite amazing. In the first place, meditating and going deep within to that transcendent space we all have the capacity of attaining stimulates the memory center of the brain. "How unexpected," you might say. True, but I don't believe that the point of the activation of our memory center is solely for the enhancement of our physical memory. Rather, in my view, this work tells us that what we're supposed to remember is that we're spiritual beings. *That's* the ultimate purpose of memory: to rekindle that deep connection between our earthly presence and the God within us.

Moreover, we now know that our genes are literally begging us to do this work. As I previously mentioned, new evidence from the white-hot forefront of molecular biology tells us that we have genes that are there to facilitate spiritual experience. In other words, we're genetically programmed to feel God's presence.

There's one final piece of science that I find very intriguing. When we meditate and go deep enough to transcend the everyday world, we increase our neurological feel-good chemicals, such as serotonin, norepinephrine, and dopamine. These are the same biopeptides that are stimulated by antidepressants such as Prozac. Depression, then, is in part nothing but the loss of the ability to elevate our self—it's merely a deficiency in the remembrance of our true self, our spirit, and our soul.

Putting This Chapter to Work in Your Life

Affirm: *Today I will again listen for the voice within, suspending any attachment or expectation of hearing it.*

My Reflections on This Chapter

_____

_____

_____

_____

_____

_____

_____

_____

✤ ✤ ✤

CHAPTER 11

Truth, Tranquility, and Wisdom

Loving this chapter grants grace.

Deeply Listening,
Truth,
Complete, utter contentment
And genuine wisdom
Will be with you
Within you.

Deeply Listening,
The purity
From bathing
In all sacred waters
Will cleanse you.

Deeply Listening,
The same honor comes

As if you had continually
Read and studied.

Deeply Listening
Brings you
To the point
Of One-Pointedness,
Flowing with the continual flow
Of the Divine Spirit
In meditative delight.

Oh my soul,
Those who surrender themselves in Love
To the Divine
Continually blossom and bloom.

Deeply Listening,
Sorrows
And errors
Depart.

Understanding This Chapter

Let's now temporarily move beyond listening to being able to feel the pulse of the Divine that is within and around you all the time. As you gain that ability, fantastic characteristics will start to seep into your being. You may even make a quantum leap in these desirable attributes, which include patience, contentment, and wisdom.

Regardless of your past actions (in this life or any other), you have the power within you to become great. It doesn't matter if you're successful; or if you're a criminal, a drug addict, or the lowest of the low in your own mind. You're ready to become exalted.

Listening to the will of God within your soul allows your spiritual labor to come to fruition. For example, you now begin to develop true intuition, which is simply the automatic knowing of what action to take in any given situation. Such action is based on your connection to your best and highest self, and when this happens, you're in the flow of life.

Putting This Chapter to Work in Your Life

Affirm: *Today I will become very conscious of my mental chatter and try to let go of the static as I focus on my deepest self.*

My Reflections on This Chapter

_____

_____

_____

_____

_____

_____

_____

_____

CHAPTER 12

Going Deeper

Meditating on this chapter gives virtues.

Deeply Listening,
Recognize
The ocean of virtues
Within you.

Deeply Listening
Become
In tune with Spirit,
Perfectly balanced
In your own humanity
And nobility.

Deeply Listening,
Even blind
You will find your way.

Deeply Listening,
Understand
The unfathomable.

Oh my soul
Those who surrender themselves in Love
To the Divine
Continually blossom and bloom.

Deeply Listening,
Sorrows
And errors
Depart.

Understanding This Chapter

Returning back to the theme of listening, this chapter tells us that by genuinely doing so, ignorant people can become wise, mere mortals can become Divine, and all creatures can transform themselves to become pure, as virtues arise in their hearts. Thus, God's love as manifested by His Will (which we hear by listening deeply) transforms ordinary folks with countless failings into saints and Godlike individuals who continually remain in bliss.

It is also restated that listening eliminates errors from our life. And this is the beginning stage of a deep, lasting, and perfect peace.

Putting This Chapter to Work in Your Life

Affirm: *Today I will continue to seek my higher self through listening and by paying greater attention to all aspects of my life.*

My Reflections on This Chapter

CHAPTER 13

Listen and Agree

*Immersing yourself in this chapter brings solidarity
of self, self-respect, and impressiveness.*

Trust what you hear
When you listen—
Even though
You won't be able
To explain it
To anyone,

And even if you do
Talk about it,
You'll just regret it
Afterwards.

There is no person
Who, with their pen,

Has the power to describe
All that is heard
When you deeply listen.

Those who sit together
And trust what they hear
When they listen
Are doing
The most powerful
Meditation.

Such is
That True Spirit
Within me
That it makes me become
Pure, clear, and sweet.

If you
Trust what you hear
When you listen,
That knowing
Becomes the psyche
Through which you
Reflect, understand,
And act.

Understanding This Chapter

With this chapter, and perhaps the preceding one as well, we see a subtle shift in the teachings. We go from an instruction to listen, to a description of the marvelous spiritual and practical benefits, and then back to listening. Now, however, the focus has shifted from simply listening to the directions given to you to agreeing to act on them. Initially, it's a subtle distinction, as you're simply told what the benefits are. In other words, you're shown the sizzle first, rather than the steak.

One who listens and agrees with what he or she hears in faith enjoys great glories beyond description. But to receive these benefits, you do have to give up a little more of your ego and favor your spiritual self. As you shall learn in the upcoming chapters, when you listen and agree, you develop an even greater sense of your true self. With that deeper sense comes the most profound understanding and awareness.

Moreover, your sense of life and even of death changes. You move beyond the fear of death that so many people carry around with them, which impedes their progress on both a spiritual and a physical plane. With time, you'll also observe that hindrances in your spiritual path vanish as your soul is enriched with honor, righteousness, and virtues—all of which lead your inner self to shine. You'll also become closer to merging with the Divine light while still in your physical form.

In essence, these chapters covering listening and agreeing with the will of God within your soul have directed you to take a great step forward. In fact, moving from hearing to believing is a leap of faith.

In Eastern terms, this ideal of devotion is called Bhakti. Bhakti is one of the paths of yoga; another with which you're probably familiar is physical yoga, or the practice of postures or *asanas*. *Yoga* means "union," and all its poses have the same purpose: the union of body, mind, and soul with the Infinite Source. Therefore, adding the power of faith and devotion to your spiritual practices will bring you all that much closer to your highest and best self. Your path to enlightenment will become accelerated, and trusting what you hear when you listen confirms the power of your inner voice.

Putting This Chapter to Work in Your Life

Affirm: *Today I will further begin to attune myself to the Divine energy and its vibration within every cell of my body. I begin to consider that I am that source.*

A lovely way to really let this sink in is to also silently repeat "I am" for ten minutes. To conclude the meditation, inhale deeply through your nose and hold your breath for five seconds. Then exhale through your nose and relax.

My Reflections on This Chapter

_____

_____

_____

_____

_____

_____

_____

_____

CHAPTER 14

Becoming Wise

*Diving into this chapter brings intuition
and the knowledge of infinity.*

By trusting
What you hear
When you listen,
The Truth
Of your own Inner
Consciousness
Will saturate your psyche
With wisdom
And deep understanding.

By trusting
What you hear
When you listen,
You shall dwell

In all mansions
Of learning.

In trusting
What you hear
When you listen,
The blows and insults
Of others
Will not affect you.

By trusting
What you hear
When you listen,
Death will have
No power over you.

Such is
That True Spirit
Within me
That it makes me become
Pure, clear, and sweet.

If you
Trust what you hear
When you listen,
Then you will know
What you see,
How to understand
And act.

Understanding This Chapter

Unquestioningly, it is faith in God and His Will as revealed in your deepest self that takes you through the journey of higher consciousness. It is the development of faith that everything is just as it's supposed to be that takes you from the darkness of materiality to the light of Divinity.

In this chapter, the exalted states of a seeker at various levels of faith are shared. When you reach the highest level of faith, where you experience the "ultimate reality" within yourself, faith ceases to be simply faith; it becomes inner experience.

This state of mind can't be described in words—it becomes a living, breathing knowledge. As you proceed on this journey, your soul will be continually cleansed from past errors and thus freed from the painful binding chains of karma. You'll then be able to transcend suffering and escape from the wheel of transmigration.

As you shall soon see, once you begin to reach this level of being, you can more easily help others on the path as well. The power of your faith, or the Word of God within you, is becoming more and more powerful.

You are very fortunate, indeed, to reach this level of spiritual existence.

Putting This Chapter to Work in Your Life

In order to practice releasing your negative emotions, feelings, and thoughts, take a deep breath and affirm (either out loud or silently): *Today I release my fears and negative thoughts. I bless them and send them back to the Universe.*

Try it whenever you have a quiet moment during the day.

My Reflections on This Chapter

CHAPTER 15

Faith

Meditating on this chapter shows you your
path, direction, and destiny in life.

In trusting
What you hear
When you listen,
There will be
No obstacles
On your path.

In trusting
What you hear
When you listen,
Radiance and honor
Will be with you.

In trusting
What you hear
When you listen,
There'll be no need
To take shortcuts
On your journey.

In trusting
What you hear
When you listen,
Dharma,
The path of Divine
Discipline and law,
Will guide
Your whole life.

Such is
That True Spirit
Within me
That it makes me become
Pure, clear, and sweet.

If you
Trust what you hear
When you listen,
That knowing
Becomes the psyche
Through which you
Reflect, understand,
And act.

Understanding This Chapter

Now you may begin to feel as if your ego is melting away. When this happens, it might seem as if you're swimming in an ocean of being—you may begin to feel the delightful presence of Divine love in your life. If you do (or perhaps more appropriately, *when* you do), then you've gathered the wonders of the inner world; consequently, you're in perfect peace, enjoying ineffable calm, supreme confidence, and total happiness. Once again, this state of experience is difficult to describe to someone who hasn't felt it for themselves. No amount of description as to how a piece of fruit tastes will ever equal the delight that the fruit actually brings.

It is your tiny self that causes illusion. But as you develop faith and devotion to the Word of God within you, you're able to more easily throw off this smaller, limited self, with all of its lower manifestations, such as anger, greed, and emotional attachment. With the release of these obstacles to spiritual growth, you're also going to be able to eliminate all the unhappiness from your life.

It should be clear from the preceding chapters that the process of conversion into the Divine isn't sudden or easy—it's the result of constant, steady effort. That's why one of my favorite sayings is: "Keep up."

You see, when you keep up with your spiritual practice through meditation in the early hours of the day, as well as prayer (and, especially, as we've seen, with listening for the Word of God within you), progress on your spiritual path is certain. So keep up and keep going onward and upward. Keep up, and you'll be kept up by the unseen hand of God.

Putting This Chapter to Work in Your Life

Affirm: *Today I recommit myself to "keeping up" with my practice of morning affirmations, prayer, and/or meditation.*

My Reflections on This Chapter

_____

_____

_____

_____

_____

_____

_____

_____

CHAPTER 16

The Thousand-Petaled Lotus

This chapter brings liberation.

Trust what you hear
When you listen
And find
The door of liberation.

Trust what you hear
When you listen,
And bring all your loved ones
Along.

Trust what you hear
When you listen.
You will swim across
All difficulties

And your very presence
Will carry others
Across as well.

And that is what it means
To be a seeker of Divine Wisdom,
Who walks from the darkness of ego
To the light
Of your own purity and spirit.

Trust what you hear
When you listen.
Even if you wander
Lost
There will be no need
To beg for anything.

Such is
That True Spirit
Within me
That it makes me become
Pure, clear, and sweet.

If you
Trust what you hear
When you listen,
Then you will know
What you see,
How to understand,
And act.

Understanding This Chapter

As you progress further along your path and develop the ability to hear the Word of God within, you begin to have an even clearer understanding of spiritual thoughts, ideas, and attitudes. You progress from knowing the truth to living it—you become a powerfully positive and passionate human being. Beyond that, as you master certain heights of spiritual energy, you're more easily able to manifest your soul-driven goals. You're also able to bring other interested people along with you, be they family members, friends, or even strangers. You can become a spiritual teacher yourself, if you like.

It's clear that you can accrue many benefits by devoting yourself to listening to the voice within, along with being able to help others on their path (which is a recurring theme of the past eight or so chapters). These countless advantages to inner communication of the soul with the Nam, or true Divine entity of the Cosmos, may be physical, moral, mental, and, of course, spiritual. Nam keeps your mind and body in a state of balance, which is clearly a highly favorable attribute to have anytime, but especially at this point in history. Peace reigns supreme when you're following your higher nature. Why? Because all of your false values, which really are the cause of so much stress and strain in your life, lose their hold on your mind, which is now free to dwell in bliss.

It may feel as if your brain is receiving the balm of a soothing massage. When you're tuned in, wasteful hurry is ended; with its departure, nervous tension and anxiety fall away, too. It's only when you realize the great pleasures found deep inside yourself, at the level of your soul, that you're able to more easily release your emotional attachment and addiction to the adrenaline rush of the outside world. When you attune your mind to the sweet music of the soul, it's relieved from the constant barrage of negative energy to which it is regularly subjected. This relief is bliss.

Another marvelous benefit of listening and agreeing is the freeing of the ego, the lower self, which tries as hard as it can to keep you from realizing your truest Divine nature. When you're able to release your ego's incredibly tenacious grasp on your mind, you're really able to enjoy life.

Many great sages call this loss of ego identification "being dead while alive." That's because when you drop the smaller self, you're then attached to the higher self. In other words, it's as if you've died and gone to heaven. You're in the light, you're liberated from the cycle of karma, and there's no more birth and death. All there is now is living in the glorious moment of the ecstasy of Divine well-being.

Your ultimate goal is to have a constant feeling of the presence of your Higher Power; in this way, the sweetness and majesty of your mystical self becomes known. And, as we shall see in the succeeding chapters, when you meet the mystical you, you can then begin to go farther in the latitude and longitude of your path to the center of your soul.

Putting This Chapter to Work in Your Life

Affirm: *Today I will take some time to contemplate all the spiritual blessings I have in my life.*

My Reflections on This Chapter

_____

_____

_____

_____

_____

_____

_____

CHAPTER 17

Formless, Peaceful, Divine

Understanding this chapter brings knowledge of the Universe.

Those who,
In the Purity of their own Spirits,
Have recognized
Their essential union with God—
They become the Living Lights
On the earth
To whom all Creation bows.

Holding the Truth of the Divine
Within their very auras,
They become True Leaders
On the earth.

In the Royal Court
Of the Divine

Those who have recognized
Their own purity
Receive the greatest honors.

Standing at the door
Of the Divine, the Supreme and Noble
Leader of leaders,
They are radiant.

The Pure Ones,
Through the Divine Teacher
Meditate
On the One.

By doing
The deepest reflection,
Still—the Doer of Doers
Cannot be
Contained
Or comprehended.

Dharma is the son of compassion,

Deep and continuous patience
Is the mantra
And the thread
Which holds it all in place
And binds everything together.

If someone understands this,
Then that person becomes
The Custodian of Truth.

How much weight
Does this son
Carry on his back?

There are so many lands,
Here and beyond.

What power is there
That supports him
And what he carries?

The names,
And the colors
Of all the different souls
Are continuously written
By the same Pen.

If someone were
To try to know Thee
By writing
All that You have
Written

How much
Writing
Would it take?

How many forms are there
Awesome in their power
And beauty?

How many gifts?

Who can know
Their limits?

With one gesture
You, oh Divine One, created
The entire Universe.

From that,
100,000 rivers
Come into being—
Currents that run through,
Nurturing the cycle of life.

What of Your
Universal, Unfathomable,
And profoundly Feminine
Creative Power
Can I speak
Or reflect?

I cannot even once
Be a sacrifice to Thee.

What pleases Thee
Is the only good
Worth doing.

Oh Divine Spirit,
You are ever
Indestructible,
Unbound, and Beyond Form.

Understanding This Chapter

Following the pulse of your Divine Inner Teacher gives you the opportunity to discover the essence of the Nam within your being. When you learn and meditate—and develop complete faith in God—you naturally and effortlessly become one with Him. When this occurs, you ceaselessly and lovingly remember Him in your heart.

When you come into this space, you look different: You're now as radiant as a young bride on her wedding day. Soon it may not be enough for you to keep this newfound ultimate reality to yourself. In one way or another, big or small, you may also want to share your experience with other seekers on the path of righteousness.

This is a fantastic idea, if it occurs to you, because in this way we'll all be able to work together for the greater good. Perhaps, by following this plan, we may be able to develop into the critical mass necessary to create the type of world we're all hoping for: one in which there is a true, just, harmonious, and lasting peace.

Putting This Chapter to Work in Your Life

Affirm: *Today I will reflect on all the progress I have made in my spiritual growth in the past year.*

My Reflections on This Chapter

_____

_____

_____

_____

_____

_____

_____

_____

CHAPTER 18

Countless

Absorbing this chapter brings freedom and resurrection.

Countless are those who call on Thee.
Countless those who Love.
Countless those who do the
Ceremonies of Fire.
Countless those who purify themselves
Through their Inner Fire.

Countless the revered and learned ones
Who recite and speak Your sacred words.

Countless those who practice Yoga,
And live detached from their own minds.

Countless those who have surrendered
Themselves

In love and devotion to Thee,
Gathering virtue, wisdom, and deep
Reflection.

Countless the respectful persons.
Countless the givers.

Countless the heroes who bear the brunt
Of battle.

Countless those who live in silence,
Attuned to Your Divine Song.

What of your
Universal, Unfathomable,
And profoundly Feminine
Creative power
Can I speak
Or reflect?

I cannot even once
Be a sacrifice to Thee.

What pleases Thee
Is the only good
Worth doing.

Oh Divine Spirit,
You are ever
Indestructible,
Beyond and Unbound by Form.

Understanding This Chapter

Although some spiritual thinkers may say that good or bad is relative, essentially a matter of opinion, this chapter gives us examples of what may be considered righteous acts. Yet it's important to realize that God, the energizer of His creation, is beyond these concepts of "goodness" or "badness."

The creative force that holds the world can't be categorized, especially in words—it just is. When you're able to suspend your thought process and transcend the limited notion of God being this or that, as opposed to God being everything, you're beginning to take yet another megastep in your spiritual evolution.

As you start to suspend your limitations where thinking of the Cosmic Truth is concerned, you begin to feel closer to all of humankind. As this happens, you begin to feel the love of the Divine in all people, and it's this love that allows you to perpetuate the presence of Him in your life.

Feeling the Divine in all brings the elevated concept of selfless service to the forefront. When you begin to feel the presence of God in all, you see that all of humanity is to be loved, served, and perhaps even worshiped. This is spiritual humanism at its finest.

As Gandhi once said, "I am endeavoring to see God through service of humanity, for I know God is neither in heaven nor down below, but in everyone."

As you shall soon see, the next few chapters revolve around the idea that the creation as a whole is a manifestation of the Creator, who resides within His creation.

Putting This Chapter to Work in Your Life

Affirm: *As I move forward in my life, I will begin to search for ways in which I can serve humanity. This can be something as simple as giving people I come in contact with a smile and a silent prayer.*

My Reflections on This Chapter

_____

_____

_____

_____

_____

_____

_____

CHAPTER 19

Speaking from
Deep Meditation

*Understanding this chapter fights madness, deep
feelings of inferiority, and self-destructive behavior.*

Countless the weak persons
Who cannot stand to see
The horrors of the world.

Countless the thieves
Who make their living
By exploiting others.

Countless those
Who use power
In the service
Of their own egos.

Countless those
Who do not tolerate
What they don't
Understand.

Countless those
Who make so many errors
Even their errors
Breed more errors.

Countless those
Who are so wretched
They spread wretchedness
Wherever they go.

Countless those
Who do not know
The Divine is within them,
And spend their lives
Turning humanity
Against each other.

Countless those
Who never find
Anything good to say
And cloud their minds
With their own negativity.

Oh my soul,
Of my own weaknesses
I speak and see.

I cannot even once
Be a sacrifice to Thee.

What pleases Thee
Is the only good
Worth doing.

Oh Divine Spirit,
You are ever
Indestructible,
Beyond and Unbound by Form.

Understanding This Chapter

In contrast to the previous chapter, here are listed traits that we may consider "bad" or "evil." Yet the message beyond the message is that the Divine is present in all: high and low, good and bad, sinners and saints, heroes and cowards, honest people and cheats, and philanthropists and murderers. All people appear as the manifestation of the same Supreme Being—we're all lit by the same fire, although the light may seem to shine brighter in some of us more than others.

Isn't it possible that someone who is considered to be the worst example of a human being has the potential to become great in the next instant? *Everyone* has Divine potential and is capable of attaining the highest spiritual state by igniting the spark of the Divine that resides within us all. Moreover, even the best of us are not entirely free from blemishes; after all, no one is perfect.

The key point to understand is that in this play of life, it's God who assumes all the roles. The Source of everything conceivable is the One—it's He who directs the play, yet remains apart. We are like actors in this little drama we call our life, but it all emanates from His Will. We simply play our parts.

Yes, it's true that people fight wars and kill each other, but this is done through absolute ignorance and insanity. If warmongers had the realization that we're all the same, wouldn't they realize that there's virtually no reason about which to fight a war? How could there be? We've all come from the same energy, at the far end of an ever-expanding Cosmos.

Putting This Chapter to Work in Your Life

Affirm: *Today I will observe people closely and try to see the same light that shines within all human beings.*

My Reflections on This Chapter

_____

_____

_____

_____

_____

_____

_____

_____

✤ ✤ ✤

CHAPTER 20

Primal Sounds

This chapter brings universal knowledge,
inspiration, and revelation.

Countless the spirits
Who come into form.

Countless their enjoyment
Of the experience.

There are so very
Many of them
I cannot know
Them all.

Countless those
Who try to speak
Of these things—

What a weight
They burden
Their own minds with.

From Beyond the Beyond
Comes the Vibration
That lives within
Every creature.

From Beyond the Beyond
Come all the Voices
That honor and praise
This wondrous thing.

From Beyond the Beyond
Comes the definition
Of wisdom,
Sacred writings,
And virtue.

From Beyond the Beyond
Comes
All that is written,
All that is spoken,
And all
Sacred Sound.

From Beyond the Beyond
Comes the Instructions
Of how to attain
Complete Union with the Divine
And surrender yourself
To the experience.

The One who does
All the writing,
No one can write anything
For Him.

Living in the Purity
Of one's own self-existence,
That is how
The True Spirit comes.

That True Spirit
Is within all things
And creates all things.

Without that True Spirit
Nothing would exist.

What of Your
Universal, Unfathomable,
And profoundly Feminine
Creative power
Can I speak
Or reflect?

I cannot even once
Be a sacrifice to Thee.

What pleases Thee
Is the only good
Worth doing.

Oh Divine Spirit,
You are ever
Indestructible,
Beyond and Unbound by Form.

Understanding This Chapter

This chapter expands the concept of the Creator God being a part of everything; in fact, He *is* everything. Primal sounds are what you hear when you listen for the Word of God within your being, and what you feel when you tune in to His Will for you. Primal sounds are the essence, or the Nam, of the Creator, and the focus of spiritual living. There is no place, no being, and no entity at all without the essence of Nam.

As the great master, Guru Nanak himself, once wrote: "It is He who works everywhere and He Himself who created illusion." When you are blessed with this realization, it is by His grace.

In the last chapter, I wrote that if people had this realization, there could never be war—there can be no hatred when one sees the essential and basic unity among us all. A line in the Upanishads exemplifies this point: "Whoever beholds all beings as the same Self and the same Self in all, does not hate anyone." How can the thought that one is good and another is bad ever be considered when there is the same all-pervading Self present in all?

This chapter also introduces a new point: The sound or name used to express God isn't as important as the expression itself. For instance, Ram, Allah, Hari, Jesus, Krishna, Eloheim, or any other names are all useful to bring you closer to Him. Language is only a vehicle you can use to express your love of the Divine—therefore, all names that help you seek Him are worthwhile. No way of seeking is more sacred than any other.

Words are holy, no matter what language they're clothed in, if they spring from a loving heart. Moreover, there is no particular place—be it Mecca, Amritsar, Jerusalem, or Rome—that's more sacred than any other.

God is present everywhere.

Putting This Chapter to Work in Your Life

Affirm: *Today I will spend at least five minutes doing something to create peace in the world.*

My Reflections on This Chapter

_____

_____

_____

_____

_____

_____

_____

CHAPTER 21

Cleaning Your Mind

This chapter wipes away your misdeeds.

When the hands, the feet,
The whole body
Becomes dirty,
Water
Washes it all away.

When clothes are stained with grime,
Soap and water
Remove the stain.

But when
Our own psyches
Are polluted with the dirt
That comes from

The errors and pain
We inflict on others,

Only our True Selves
Can restore us
To our Original Color.

The virtuous,
The unvirtuous,
What a person says
Does not determine
Who he is.

It is the actions we perform
Over and over again
That get recorded
And go along with us.

What seeds I sow,
That food
I have to eat.

Oh my soul,
In the Will of the Divine,
We come and we go.

Understanding This Chapter

If you're like most people, for the greatest part of your life your soul has probably been wandering around under the control of your mind and senses. Until you were blessed to seriously consider your spiritual development, you've more than likely been cast about by the impressions you've taken into your mind from the outside world. You may have identified yourself with your body and your ego—thus, you've forgotten much of your true self (until recently), with which you're now becoming acquainted.

Perhaps you've been carried away by a business success, which brought you a lot of money. With this achievement came a bigger home, a nicer car, and other trappings of wealth . . . yet you may have forgotten your soul while you focused on the material aspects of life. Maybe you also forgot that all of your success came from God. No matter; as you've seen, the most effective way to remove this type of negative thinking from your mind is to dwell on your Higher Power with love and devotion. This is how to end your karma.

When it comes to karma, however, many people revert back to thinking about "good karma" or "bad karma." Yet, as we're learning, there's really no such thing. The consideration of actions, whether thought to be good or bad, fails to bring you much closer to your depth, because it keeps you attached or focused on the outer-centered world rather than on your innermost soul.

It was Lord Krishna who once said: "Good or bad actions are fetters, which equally bind the soul to the world, irrespective of whether they are of gold or of iron."

It's entirely possible that your mind may have been polluted by some of the actions you've taken on your path. But your mind—and your soul—can be cleansed by the love of the Nam, which resides within and is discovered by your regular spiritual practice, and by reading this book.

Your current actions, motivated by your higher values, will clear away the mist of a troubled mind. It's then that your Divinity can shine forth in its full glory. By meditating deeply on the essence of the Creator in the early hours of the morning, your mind will be restored to its original transparency.

There is no more wonderful sanctuary for you during the storm of today's age of intensity, anxiety, and insanity than a purified mind.

Putting This Chapter to Work in Your Life

Affirm: *Today, again, I will rededicate myself to getting in touch with my highest self. I will do so by taking the time to read this book and meditate first thing in the morning. I will tune in to the Word of God within my being and keep that feeling of connection with me during the busy hours of the day.*

If I lose that feeling, I may return to that vibration by taking a nice, long, slow, deep breath and exhaling with the silent inner sound of Sat Nam, which means "my true self."

My Reflections on This Chapter

_____

_____

_____

_____

_____

_____

_____

_____

❖ ❖ ❖

CHAPTER 22

Let Love Fill Your Mind

*Living this chapter will maintain your
status, grace, and position.*

Sacred baths,
Practices of the Inner Fire,
Kindness,
Giving gifts—
Even if someone
Has the consciousness
To do these things,
It will only bring
A sesame seed's worth
Of honor.

Deeply Listening,
Trusting what you hear when you listen,

Let your mind
Be kindled
In love.

Find the sacred bathing place
Within your own self
And wash off
The filth.

All virtues are Yours,
My Beloved.
Of my own,
I have none at all.

And without Your virtues
Devotion to You
Is not even possible.

I am enamored of Thee,
Oh Primal One—
Beyond Time and Space
Who, through Your Word,
Brings the Creative Forces
Of the Universe into play.

What was that time?
What epoch?
What phase of the moon?
What day of the sun?
What season?
What month?

When the Formless
Took Form?

The spiritual scholars
Have never figured it out,
And they have said as much
In their sacred books.

The season and the day
Is not known
By the Yogis.

The season and the month
Is not known by anyone.

When did the Great Creator
Form the earth
With His Hands?
Only He, Himself,
Knows.

How can I
Find the words?
How can I honor and praise it?
How can I picture it?
How can I even
Know it?

Oh my soul,
With words,
Everyone talks about it—

Each person
Trying to be
More clever and wise
Than the last.

Great is the Master,
Great is His Spirit within me,
Created by His own Command.

Oh my soul,
If anybody
Within themselves
Thinks they know You,
There will be nothing for them
When they die.

Understanding This Chapter

Taking trips to holy lands should be saluted if they enable you to advance on your spiritual path. (Many people make pilgrimages to special places in India, for example, where they may bathe in holy water.) This type of endeavor can help you end your karma if it creates a greater awareness of the inner Nam.

One of the key points of this chapter, however, is that you can receive the same benefits of a pilgrimage—and take a holy bath inside yourself—when the love of the true essence of your higher self is fostered to grow within your heart and mind. As a great sage once said, "One takes a holy bath within oneself when one recognizes the True One."

When you grow to love the essence of your highest self and feel it vibrating, pulsating, or ringing within the deepest recesses of your soul, you don't have to go anywhere to purify your soul. You can sit in your living room and enjoy a deep inner-spiritual cleansing by focusing your mind on the Nam. When you begin to feel the love of your true essence within yourself, you're going to a place of immortality in your own being. You're getting a deep and lasting spiritual knowledge. It is this powerful experience that we all seek, and which is the nature and purpose of our existence.

Unfortunately, the opposite is also true. Perhaps you've seen someone who, despite their trips to holy places or devotion to their religious practices, remains shallow. Their karma continues to take its toll; therefore, any devotional practice they undertake is ineffective because it fails to generate spiritual power.

Spiritual power comes through inner purification; and by living a virtuous life of truth, love, humility, and compassion. For you to end your karma, a life of continual positive right action must be undertaken. The benefits of living such a royal life are so worthwhile that any effort you may have had to make to get there is well worth it. As Cicero felt: "Virtue draws people to true honor by its own charm." In other words, once you begin to experience the benefits of living a committed spiritual life, you won't want to live any other way.

The second part of this chapter tells us that no one, despite all their academic or intellectual pursuits, has any knowledge of the actual workings of the Cosmos. It is the Creator alone who knows when He Himself fashioned the world and how it runs. And we're again reminded that our primary guiding principle of spiritual existence is not to worry about these matters. We may admire them and wonder in their amazement, but we can't count them or truly understand the way of the Creator. That would be like reducing the infinite to the finite—it simply can't be done with our limited human ingenuity.

Nor is this kind of understanding necessary for progress in the spiritual realm. You don't have to be diverted from the essence of your Divinity to matters that are irrelevant to your own spiritual growth. All you have to do to grow rich spiritually is stay in touch with your Higher Power, the Nam, and live in that ecstasy.

Putting This Chapter to Work in Your Life

Affirm: *Today I will spend 15 minutes in absolute silence to feel the presence of my Higher Power.*

My Reflections on This Chapter

_____

_____

_____

_____

_____

_____

_____

_____

✧✧✧

CHAPTER 23

Only He Knows

This chapter brings strategy and victory.

There are worlds and worlds
Below us.

There are worlds and worlds
Above us.

In the end,
In the end
You'll grow tired
Searching them all.

The sacred scriptures
Say this
With one voice.

There are 18,000 worlds,
The various scriptures say,
Countless worlds.

But the Source Beyond the Source
Is only One.
Writing this down,
It becomes a written record.

But in time
What is written
Will be destroyed.

Oh my soul,
What is truly great
Is to know Yourself.

Understanding This Chapter

All the holy books tell us of the many, many, aspects of creation. Yet they all also tell us that there is just One Creator. Always remember that the "goal" of your good spiritual work is to discover your best self and to live in concert with that energy. That is perhaps the best way to praise your Creator.

It is only He Himself who knows the vastness of His existence. Your job is to discover your own vastness as a spiritual human being.

Putting This Chapter to Work in Your Life

Affirm: *Today I will take five to ten minutes before going to work to consider my own vastness.*

My Reflections on This Chapter

_____

_____

_____

_____

_____

_____

_____

CHAPTER 24

Never Forget Your Maker

Meditating on this chapter dispels darkness and elevates the self.

Those in a state of joy
Praise Thee.
Yet, in this manner
True Spiritual Understanding
Is not given or received.

Streams and rivers
Flow along,
Not knowing
They are merging
Into the Ocean.

That Ocean
Is the Great, True
Noble Ruler

Who guards the wealth
And jewels
Of spiritual learning.

Even an ant
Is not left behind
If he never forgets God
From his mind.

Understanding This Chapter

As great as we may be, we're nothing if we don't remember
our Creator. We have no idea how vast the latitude and
longitude of creation is. We're only a moment's sunlight
fading in the horizon while the creation goes on and on.
We're just a drop of water flowing from a stream into a river
and then onward into the sea.

Keep in mind the following words:

Endless are God's excellences.
Endless are His expressions.
Endless His doings.
And endless are His gifts.

It is virtually impossible to fathom the purpose of His
total will, unless you're also that high. And no one is.

Putting this into context, and thinking about it, perhaps
you can reflect upon His glance of grace, which you've
received, and the gifts He has given to you.

Putting This Chapter to Work in Your Life

Today, write down all the gifts you've been given by the Creator. Perhaps you can tape your list of blessings to your bathroom mirror so that you can see and remember them every day. Make another list of the worthy goals you'd like to complete, and put them in a conspicuous place and read them often.

My Reflections on This Chapter

_____

_____

_____

_____

_____

_____

_____

_____

CHAPTER 25

There Is No End in Sight

*This chapter breaks through all limitations
with the force of a thunderbolt. It has the power
to eliminate misfortunes for generations.*

There is no end
To all that You
Create and do.

What we can
Say about You,
There's no end to that, either.

There is no end
To Your actions.

And to what
You give
There is no end.

There is no end
To what we see.

And to what we hear
There is no end.

There is no end
To the visions created
By You coming
Into Form.

There is no end.
The visions go on
As far as we can see.

There is a limit
To our understanding
Of Thee.

How many veils
Like this
Do we have to go through?

There is no end
To Thee, my Beloved.

This is the understanding
I've received
And go along with.

This Unending
Anybody can know.

The more we talk,
The more there is to say.

Great is the Master
In the Highest Place.

Even Higher still
Is His Spirit
Within me.

Any person
Can be
In this height.

And in this height,
You will know God.

How great You are
And how great it is
To know You.

Oh Seeker of Spirit,
Grace and karma
Are both Thy gifts.

Understanding This Chapter

The key point to take from this chapter is fairly simple: The Creator's creation is limitless. Many authors, thinkers, and spiritual philosophers have tried to fathom its mystery, yet no one can really know God until they reach His height. And, as I've stated so many times, no human being can or ever will.

Your soul will behold God only when you reach the highest of spiritual planes. Masters call this dimension "Sach Khand," or the stage of truth. Most mortal beings actually have to die and leave their physical body in order to approach this state of being, also called "nirvana" by Buddhists.

Others may have a near-death experience (NDE) in which they're touched by a Higher Power, perhaps a vision of Jesus or Moses or Buddha, and given the blessing of deep inner knowing and sublime inner peace.

But what about the rest of us? Well, we are what is known as "householders." A householder is someone who is on a serious spiritual quest but lives in the everyday working world. Because we're spiritual, however, I don't consider us regular. Regular folks are those who get up in the morning and go to work or live their life as it is, *without* taking the time to tune in to their highest self via spiritual practice such as meditation or prayer.

When I observe people without a spiritual life, I feel sadness and compassion. No matter how beautiful they are, how much money they have, or how wonderful their children become, I see deep stress, conflict, and unhappiness. Sometimes it's just below the surface, and sometimes it's buried very deeply inside them, but to my second sight it's there nonetheless. Sadly, these individuals don't even have a clue that they're spiritually deficient until they're on their deathbed. And then they have a lot of karma to work out at the end of their life.

From my professional life as a physician (and as someone who, unfortunately, has lost family members both young and quite old), I can tell you that a person's karma has to be cleared before he or she can check out of this world. I particularly remember one individual who struggled greatly for the last months of her life. She kept reliving events and resolving issues in her mind before she finally just told her family, "I'm ready to go." She'd worked out what she'd needed to, and when she was done she was able to move to the great beyond. She was then able to transcend to her next level of existence.

My hope is that this won't happen to you. I pray every day for each person on this planet to be blessed with living a spiritual life. How else will we be able to behold the highest truth with our material eyes? We must all transcend on the wings of His Will, and we can only do so through His Grace.

Putting This Chapter to Work in Your Life

I'd like you to meditate upon the following: A debate currently rages among scientists about the origin of the Universe and all of the species in it. But if the creation appears as only a manifestation of His Will—and His Will is expressing itself in the creation, through the creative process—then what is the significance of these intellectual discussions? Do you think there is one?

My Reflections on This Chapter

_____

_____

_____

_____

_____

_____

_____

_____

CHAPTER 26

There Is So Much Karma

Mastering this chapter fulfills all your needs. Prosperity,
virtue, estate, and wealth are yours without asking.

There are so many
Karmic plays,
It isn't possible
To write them all.

The Great Giver
Withholds nothing—
Not even the tiniest
Sesame seed.

There are so many warriors
Begging to merge into Thee.
There are so many
Who are counting

But never
Reflect on or see You.

So many are exhausted
Having broken themselves
On vice.

There are so many
Who take everything
And then deny
Receiving.

So many foolish ones
Do nothing but
Stuff their face
With food.

So many are
Continually beaten down
By endless pain and hunger.

Even these
Are your Gifts to us
Great Giver.

Slavery.
Freedom.
Both come
From You.

It isn't possible
For anyone
To say more
Than this.

If someone
Who likes the sound
Of his own voice
Tries to speak
About this,

He'll be shamed
In so many ways.

You, Yourself, know.
You, Yourself, give.

Those who can speak of it
This way
Are very few.

The ones You bless
To meditatively and lovingly
Chant and sing
Your wonders,

Oh Seeker of Spirit
Those persons
Are the nobility
Of nobility.

Understanding This Chapter

This chapter is yet another demarcation point for the next level of deep spiritual thought. It's deep because we rarely think of these concepts—yet when we do, what's seen is that while they may have profound significance, they're incredibly practical as well.

When my spiritual teacher (His Holiness The Siri Singh Sahib, Yogi Bhajan) embarked on his journey to America in 1969, he said a prayer and asked God for a sign. This chapter is the message he received. He said that at that point he knew he'd be very successful, but he also realized that he'd have to go through many challenges in his new life. And both of these things did come to pass.

The reality is that we're all given so much in our life by Him—His bounty is supreme. Because He is so magnanimous, He showers His gifts on all alike, regardless of their so-called goodness and badness or high or low station. Everyone gets their share; none are ignored.

This chapter shows us that, like some of our earthly parents, the Divine energy that put you here on Earth knows you better than you know yourself, and it bestows upon you what's needed and what's best. The problem is that very few people ever have this thought: *I am blessed.*

When you have that realization, you may consider yourself to have received the gift of eternal life. When this blessing is confirmed upon you, out of His grace, you are among the highest of the high.

Putting This Chapter to Work in Your Life

Affirm: *Today I think about how some of my most difficult times turned out to be, in retrospect, an important jumping-off spot for a quantum leap in my spiritual growth, financial success, personal health, or happiness.*

My Reflections on This Chapter

CHAPTER 27

Priceless

Owning this chapter often transforms nothing into everything.
It banishes losses, misfortunes, and miseries.

Beyond Price
Are Your virtues.

Beyond Price
Is trading
In Your virtues.

Beyond Price
Are those who live
By trading
In Your virtues.

Beyond Price
Is the storehouse,

The body,
Where these treasures
Are kept.

Beyond Price
Are those who come
Looking to purchase
Your virtues.

Beyond Price
Is what they
Take away with them
When they go.

Beyond Price
Is the experience
Of surrendering ourselves
To the Divine
Through Love.

Beyond Price
Is the acceptance
Of the Divine
And living
In that complete embrace.

Beyond Price
Is Your Spiritual Law.

Beyond Price
Is the Court
Where that law
Is practiced.

Beyond Price
Is the Divine Assessment
Where our Purity
Is measured like gold.

Beyond Price
Is that moment when,
By God's Grace,
Our Purity reigns.

Beyond Price
Is the avalanche
Of blessings and gifts
That come to us
At that moment.

Beyond Price
Is being a public sign
Of the sovereignty and dignity
Of the Divine Spirit.

Beyond Price
Are our own actions.

Beyond Price
The Divine Will
Which directs them.

Oh—so far beyond
Any price
Are these things,
There's no way
To speak of it.

Talking and talking,
We grow tired.

Stay attuned
To the Truth.

Those who recite sacred texts
Talk.

The scholars,
Creating so many descriptions,
Talk.

Brahma talks.
Indra talks.
The devotees of Krishna talk.
Shiva talks.
The intense yogis talk.
So many elders talk.
Desperate souls talk.
Minor gods and goddesses talk.

Saints, ascetic wanderers,
Those who meditate alone,
Those who serve others
Talk.

So many talk.
So many others
Try to talk.

And after all these people
Talk and talk,
They die and die
Going their way.

The Divine made them all.

And the Divine
Will make
So many more.

Those
Who have nothing to say
Are very few.

As great
As You want us to be
Oh Divine Spirit,

That great
You make us.

Oh my soul—
There is only
The One True One.

If someone speaks,
They are misleading
Through words,
And everyone will recognize them
As the fool of all fools.

Understanding This Chapter

Here we continue to contemplate the often-under-appreciated gifts we all receive, which are absolutely priceless. How much is your next breath worth? How much would you pay for this human birth, the purpose of which is to come to know your True Creator as well as possible, and thus clear your karma so that you can merge in His light? Is there a value you can assign to that?

Not only that, but think about this: Each of your gifts is totally unique. A very special energy has taken the time to give you the attention you deserve so that you can become your true and best self during this lifetime. You don't get anything close to what I get, and what I receive is certainly different from what you're given. And it's all for quite a good reason.

God is unique and peerless in His actions. One person may be born very tall and athletic so that he or she can express His Will by being a great basketball player. When interviewed by the press, this person may actually acknowledge his or her great gifts and give God the credit. Another person with similar athletic abilities may be born short so that he or she can become a scientist and perhaps discover the cure for a serious illness. You just never know.

Many people throughout the ages have sung His praises and continue to do so. Countless more to come undoubtedly shall do the same. Nevertheless, the workings of the Almighty have remained incomprehensible by mortal humans forever.

Putting This Chapter to Work in Your Life

Please take five to ten minutes to seriously imagine how you've been given unique gifts that have been exactly what you need to get you through this life. Now spend the rest of today breathing deeply and being extremely grateful.

My Reflections on This Chapter

_____

_____

_____

_____

_____

_____

_____

CHAPTER 28

In What House?

Meditating on this chapter removes obstacles and hurdles.
It shows you the way when you're stuck.

Where is that door,
What is that home
In which You sit
And look after everything?

There are so many
Countless
Subtle melodies
Which call the Creation
Into Being,
Weaving together
In harmony.

How many souls there are
That carry and express
The music.

How many subtle beings
And spirits there are
Who continuously practice
Your Divine Scales.

How many singers there are
Who sing along with Thee.

Air, Water, and Fire
Sing to You.

In singing, Thou,
Oh Noble Ruler
Of Spiritual Law
Come to our door.

The beings that record
Our thoughts and deeds
Sing to You,
And, in singing, record
Our actions for all to know.

In this record,
Spiritual Law
Sees clearly
What we are.

The Creative Forces
Of the Universe,
Beautiful and
Always bejeweled,
Sing to You.

The Forces
That govern the Seasons
From the Heavens
Sing to You,

As do the Natural Forces
On the Earth.

The perfected Spiritual Persons
Who ever remain
In Divine Union with Thee
Sing to You.

As do the Disciplined Ones
Who spend their time
In reflection and meditation.

Men and women
Of Moral Self-restraint,
Of Truth
And of Contentment
Sing to You,

As do the Strong
And Noble Heroes.

Learned persons,
Scholars,
And Spiritual masters
Sing to You,

As do
All the Books of Learning
Throughout the ages.

All the enchanting
Visions
Which attract
And enrapture the mind
In the Heavens,
On the Earth,
And Below
Sing to You.

All the jewels
Created by You
Sing to You,

As do all
The Sacred Places.

The brave and courageous Warriors
Sing to You,

As do the Four Treasures
Of Peace, Contentment,
Love, and Divine Union.

All the Universes and Galaxies,
Planets in the Solar Systems,
All the Continents
In all the Lands
Sing to You,

And as You continually
Make them,
You protect and support them.

Those who sing to You
Are those who are
Pleasing to You.

They are
Permeated through
With surrendered Love
And become
The Keepers of Thy Essence.

There are so many more
Who sing to You,
I can't even
Think of them all.

Oh my soul,
How can I even
Talk about it?

Thou, oh Thou
You are always
The True One,
The Master of All.

Truth Pervading.
True Spirit in Form.

You shall ever be—
Though nothing You created
Will go along
With You.

Every color,
Every unique thing,
Is continually made
By You.

You who created
All the elements,
And the Divine Cosmic Play
That comes from them,
Creating and creating,
You, Yourself,
Enjoy
What You have done.

And this
Is Your greatness.

You do
What pleases You.

There is nowhere
Your Divine Will
Doesn't prevail.

Oh True Emperor,
Divine King,
Noble of the Noble,

My soul lives
Surrendered to Your Command.

Understanding This Chapter

The theme is advancing again, so I'm glad that you took the time to breathe deeply after the last chapter—you're going to need the clarity it brought you. Perhaps you were able to breathe deeply for this chapter as well.

For a moment, please imagine or visualize what it might be like to be the sole powerful, creative, energetic force that holds the world together and resides in every corner of the Universe. Imagine for a moment how God might feel as He is looking upon all of creation. Here in this spot is everyone who has ever sung His praises. The language is extremely lyrical, and the energy is unparalleled!

What's important for you to absorb at the moment is that it's possible for you to be in such a place. To get there requires that you take the time in your life to sing His praises. You can do that out loud at a ceremony or a service of your choice, or by singing silently inside yourself. The ultimate idea is to remember Him with every breath. That's your dharma, which ends your karma.

I believe that the operative word here ought to be *genuine*. If you decide to believe in God and worship Him, it can't be because you read it in a book or someone said that it was the right thing to do. This may make you feel good temporarily, but it won't provide you with any long-term benefit or progress on your path.

What you have to do in your own way is take the time to tune in to His vibration, interpret it, and uniquely live it. This is the greatest truth there is. Everything else, however highly thought of, is subservient to His Will.

God remains the same throughout all time. He never changes.

Putting This Chapter to Work in Your Life

Meditate deeply, and mentally place yourself at the feet of God in His court. What does it feel like to be one with Him? Please take a little extra time, say 15 minutes or so, to do this exercise. Then try to merge yourself in that energy and keep it with you during the day.

My Reflections on This Chapter

_____

_____

_____

_____

_____

_____

_____

❖ ❖ ❖

CHAPTER 29

Conquer Your Mind and You'll Conquer the World

This chapter unites you with God.

May you wear
The earrings
Of deep contentment.

May humility
Be your begging bowl
And the shawl in which
You carry your belongings.

May being centered
In the center of your being
Be the ashes
That cleanse you.

Wear the patched coat
Of Death.

Keep your body pure,
Like a virgin.

And may the staff
That holds you upright
As you walk along your journey
Be the constant remembrance
Of Spirit within you.

Let the highest
And best company
Be the brotherhood and sisterhood
Of all peoples.

Conquer your mind
To conquer the world.

I bow
To the very act
Of bowing to Thee,
Oh Divine One.

Beyond Time.
Beyond Color.
Beyond Sound.
Beyond Form and Containment.

Age after Age,
You are the One.

Understanding This Chapter

Please allow me to call your attention to the stated benefit of reading, meditating upon, and understanding this particular chapter. If you can immerse yourself in these words, you'll be united with God. When you earn a victory over your ego by focusing on your spirit, you'll surely prosper in your life, both materially and spiritually. Your karma will end.

Following a life of true devotion is preferable to living one of ritual. The type of life that's required to reach His door is one of inner discipline, rather than of outer trappings. The action of lovingly singing His praises again and again during your life brings your soul great honor and your spirit tremendous energy. That is all God wants from you—nothing more and nothing less. He just wants you to think of Him.

Remember, we're all the same: We're all created in the image of God. People may be of many types, but humanity is one. In spite of our differences of race, color, sex, nationality, religion, and circumstances of living, everyone's spiritual needs are essentially the same. It's only when we forgo outside trappings and adorn ourselves with contentment, faith, purity, self-control, and honest work that we enter the temple of the soul. This is how our spiritual practice will yield real fruit, and the development of these virtues is how we can actually measure our progress on the path.

All genuine seekers on the path are members of the same invisible church and are colleagues in the effort to nourish their spiritual lives. As mere mortals, we're all subject to the same spiritual laws, including those of karma. Only God is beyond karma. When you truly get this, you have taken yet another giant leap in your spiritual development.

So, then, how is it possible to end your karma? You can do so by giving your wholehearted allegiance, loyalty, and devotion to Him. That's when you're able to "know thyself." Self-realization is the aim of life and, as the self of all selves, resides in your soul. True self-knowledge comes from meditation on the One.

This is the royal road to the perfect peace, tranquility, and joy that you seek.

Putting This Chapter to Work in Your Life

Affirm: *Today I will take a moment to mentally identify and put aside any false or ritualistic spiritual ideas or practices, if any, I might have. I ask myself if perhaps there is one action I can take today to bring myself closer to my own highest self and hence God.*

My Reflections on This Chapter

_____

_____

_____

_____

_____

_____

_____

_____

❖ ❖ ❖

CHAPTER 30

I Salute Him Over and Over Again

This chapter grants you protection from animosity.

Nourish yourself
Along your journey
With morsels
Of wisdom.

Let kindness
Bear your burdens
For you,
As the beat of God's Command
Vibrates
In your every
Heartbeat.
Thy, Thyself,

Are the Master.

All else
Follows Thee.

Occult powers
Taste false.

The Great Divine Union,
The Preordained Separation,
Both Forces
Run the entire Universe.

I bow
To the very act
Of bowing to Thee,
Oh Divine One.

Beyond Time.
Beyond Color.
Beyond Sound.
Beyond Form and Containment.

Age after Age,
You are the One.

Understanding This Chapter

Advancing the theme of the last few chapters, this one emphasizes that there is just one God, and it's your job as a spiritual seeker to salute Him over and over again. That is the supreme purpose of life. Unfortunately, many people, even those on a spiritual path, take more pleasure in wealth and power than in realizing their Divine inner nature.

Today, the practice of yoga is becoming more and more popular. Some people enjoy it because of the trim body they obtain by doing it on a regular basis, others like the way it makes them feel, and still others use it to help heal themselves of an illness. (An actual yogi may also develop incredible physical and mental powers called *siddhis*.) The ultimate purpose of yoga, however, is the union of body, mind, and spirit with the Divine Force. As individuals advance on their spiritual path by doing yoga, they come to understand on a very profound level that the benefits they obtain from their practice are all a gift from the Creator. Everything is heaven-sent.

What you can learn by reading and meditating upon this chapter, therefore, is that all your gifts in this life come from Him, and it's your actions on a daily basis that determine if you reach your true destiny in this short time you have on Earth, or merely settle for the occurrence of your fate.

Once again, you can see that the answer is really quite simple: To reach your goal of spiritual realization requires you to salute Him regularly through meditation, prayer, or chanting. God has no equal in money, fame, sex, or power. Through all time, there is only the One.

May you never forget Him . . . not even for an instant.

Putting This Chapter to Work in Your Life

Affirm: *Today, with every breath I take, I allow myself to connect with God.*

My Reflections on This Chapter

_____

_____

_____

_____

_____

_____

_____

_____

CHAPTER 31

Through All Ages

Reading this chapter places you upon the throne
of Divinity. It makes you a saint and a sage.

There is One Mother
Married
To all time and space.

From Her,
Three Devotees
Are born.

One that creates.
One that nourishes.
One that holds court, deciding the fate.

As it pleases Thee, oh Divine One,
So these devotees move,

Acting according to Thy Divine
Command.

The Divine
Sees all.

But the created
Can't see the Divine
At all.

Wow!
This is such
A great drama.

I bow
To the very act
Of bowing to Thee,
Oh Divine One.

Beyond Time.
Beyond Color.
Beyond Sound.
Beyond Form and Containment.

Age after age,
You are the One.

Understanding This Chapter

As you can probably tell, the theme of God being the doer of everything (and our main spiritual task being to salute Him) is a very crucial concept of advanced spiritual thought. For that reason, it's repeated many times in this section of the book. If this concept hasn't become apparent to you yet, by the time you finish this section of chapters, it will be very clear.

The Creator does all, and moves the world as He wishes. Yet He is so vast that no one can see, understand, or know Him *in toto*. You may get a glance, or have a feeling or an inner experience, but no one can ever come close to fully understanding His wonder. The only way to come close is by His grace, and that comes by singing His praises, becoming pure, and living a life of truth.

He is the pure light, the primal being—eternal, immortal, and forever. Everything that's ever been created, as well as everything that is sustained over time (including you) or eventually passes, does so according to His Will.

Life is to be considered an opportunity to serve Him by serving humanity, and to realize Him by feeling His presence in the depths of your being.

Putting This Chapter to Work in Your Life

Affirm: *Today I shall take the time to try to come to the realization that there's no limit to Divine abundance. I visualize total health and prosperity coming to me now.*

My Reflections on This Chapter

_____

_____

_____

_____

_____

_____

_____

_____

CHAPTER 32

One Soul

This chapter gives you heavenly virtues.

You have Your thrones
On every world.

And in every world
You've placed
Your treasures.

Whatever was placed there
By You
Was placed
Once and for all.

Oh Spirit of Union and Connection,
You look out for

All You continually
Make and do.

The True One
Creates
The True Creation.

I bow
To the very act
Of bowing to Thee
Oh Divine One.

Beyond Time.
Beyond Color.
Beyond Sound.
Beyond Form and Containment.

Age after age,
You are the One.

Understanding This Chapter

Your highest, best sense of self, that familiar place deep inside your soul, contains the same energy that is everywhere in the Cosmos. How could it be any other way? We're all one with the infinity of Divinity; we're all one with the One. Perhaps you've never been taught that so completely before—it may have always been more of a passing thought. It's also possible that this idea was something that you knew intuitively, but if you're like most people, you've never dwelled on this accepted wisdom completely enough to make it your own.

Upon your birth, God gave you the feeling of separation from Him. No one knows why. You came from a place of light and deep meditation into this world of action, and you've been led into an existence of attachment to the sensuous phenomena of the world. So long as you remain aware of the Divinity diffused in the world, however, you'll also be aware of Him residing within you.

Yet when petty ego cuts you off from your Divine self and you assert your independent mind and begin to believe that you're the active agent of your life, you get trapped right back in the cycle of karma. This may translate as emotional pain, suffering, and misery, until you rejuvenate your soul by again developing within yourself a deep desire for inner peace, and rededicate your life to that end. That's when you'll uncover your highest self and find true contentment.

This ends your karma and brings you in touch with your highest destiny: knowing God's Will for you and dwelling in His vibratory essence.

Putting This Chapter to Work in Your Life

Affirm: *Today I pay attention to the moments of peace I experience, as opposed to the moments of stress.*

My Reflections on This Chapter

_____

_____

_____

_____

_____

_____

_____

_____

CHAPTER 33

Twenty Million Tongues

*Meditating deeply on this chapter pays your
debts and completes your karma.*

If my one tongue
Were to become two,
And the two to become
One million,
And the million
To become twenty million,

Then millions and millions
Of times
I would recite and speak
Of the One Spirit
Pervading and guiding
The Universe.

On this path,
The spouse climbs
With devotion
Step by step
To Union with Thee.

Hearing what is recorded
In the Akashic records,
Even the lowest beings
Have a longing
To return home.

Oh my soul,
Grace is brought in
As a gift of the Creator.

Those who praise themselves—
False are they
And ever false.

Understanding This Chapter

Sometimes it's imperative to repeat an important point. In this chapter, an essential spiritual idea is emphasized. Are you taking the time to think about it, or are you running through it by saying something like, "Oh, I know this, why dwell on it again"?

In case your concentration is wandering, let's review a bit so that you can more fully grasp the points that are being made.

Communion with your highest self, the God within, the essence of which is called the Nam or your true identity, is also referred to as "Sat Nam." The expression of the Nam in you is hindered by your earthly desires. These issues pull at your heart and mind and lead you away from the truth within your being to the outside world.

How then are you to overcome these illusionary desires? This chapter tells you again, perhaps in a different way, that the answer is in constant remembrance of your higher self, or the God within. Spiritual masters often call this "simran," or repetition of the Nam. This repetition, or constant remembrance of God, is the way to be liberated from your karma and merge with Him.

Genuine advanced yogis, swamis, and monks (perhaps erroneously) believe that the way to ending karma is by withdrawing their energy from the material world. But through simran or constant remembrance of God via meditation on the Nam, this withdrawal of attention to the world is unnecessary. In fact, as mentioned previously, it's more powerful for you as a Westerner to be in the "normal," workaday world. It's more natural for you to live this way, with family responsibilities and so forth, than to remove yourself from your temporal obligations to go and live in a cave somewhere or stay on constant retreat.

In a sense, when you meditate on the Nam and practice simran, you do withdraw your senses from the spurious characteristics of materialism and ego to focus on your highest self. Once you've learned this easy and natural technique of sensory withdrawal (which I'll explain later on and suggest you try in the section below), your soul will advance further on the spiritual path.

In the Bible it is suggested that the way to the Creator is to learn to die so that you may begin to live. In other words, by focusing your energy on your Higher Power, you're essentially removing your attention from the world, even though you're living and acting in it. That is the beginning of the next, more advanced phase of spiritual living.

The ultimate recollection to have, however, is this: To achieve the end of karma requires not only effort—it also requires His Grace and Will.

Putting This Chapter to Work in Your Life

Simran is a shift of consciousness to a higher level. To experience it, follow these steps:

1. Close both of your eyes, inhale deeply through your nose, hold your breath, and focus your attention behind your eyes at the seat of your soul. Roll your eyes up slightly as you do this.

2. While holding your breath, say "Sat Nam" three times. Then exhale through your nose.

3. Inhale and repeat the process a total of five times.

4. On the final exhalation, hold your breath out for a count of five. Next, inhale through your nose, holding the breath for a count of five as you meditate on the feeling or energy you've generated.

5. Now exhale and relax.

6. Go back to your normal breathing, but whenever you want to remember Him during the day, repeat this process of simran.

My Reflections on This Chapter

_____

_____

_____

_____

_____

_____

_____

_____

✣ ✣ ✣

CHAPTER 34

No Power

*Understanding this chapter destroys ego, removes
negativity, and neutralizes destructiveness.*

The power to speak
Or keep silent—
I don't have that power.

I don't have the power
To beg or to give.

When I live,
When I die—
Is far beyond my power.

I have no power
To rule as a King

With wealth,
Or through the force
Of my own mental manipulations.

I have no power
To attach myself to God through
Meditation,
Or to attain wisdom,
Or to reflect on what I see.

I have no power
To know the way
To liberate myself
From the world.

Whose Hand
Holds this power?

The One
Who does and sees all.

Oh my soul,
No one is high
And no one is low.

Understanding This Chapter

This short chapter, in my experience, is one of the most important and powerful in *The End of Karma*. I've reread it many times, and I can't begin to tell you how many benefits it's given me. For one thing, meditating on it has helped me to eliminate a lot of negativity and, as it says above, to neutralize destructiveness. It's brought me great gifts of God's blessing and love.

Essentially, this chapter concludes the previous section by summarizing what has been discussed: God has all the power, and when we receive a gift, it's by His grace. In all matters—in fact, in every single thing—His Will is all.

To let go of your previous conceived notions of the way things are, and to realize this idea in its entirety, will get you yet another step closer to the end of your karma by bringing you to "at-one-ment" or union with God.

Putting This Chapter to Work in Your Life

Today, begin to understand more fully that all of your power—and all of your success and happiness—comes from the Supreme Ultimate Source. When you've completed this book, I hope that you have the opportunity to return to this chapter over and over again. I believe that we can all profit greatly from the benefits offered by its understanding.

My Reflections on This Chapter

_____

_____

_____

_____

_____

_____

_____

_____

CHAPTER 35

Grace Covers Your Karma

By meditating on this chapter, you gain stability.

Nights, seasons,
Moon cycles, days.

Wind, water,
Fire, and the underworld,

In the midst of this,
The Earth was established
As a place
Where Spirit could evolve
Into a Conscious Awareness of Itself,
Protected.

For that purpose,
The souls came

Through time and space
In such a variety
Of colors.

Those souls
Are so many,
They are countless.

There are actions
Upon actions
And we reflect
On what we do.

Thou, oh Divine One,
Is True
And True
Is Your Royal Court
In which all
Is contained.

In Your Royal Court,
Your devotees,
The ones who have found themselves
Within themselves,
Look beautiful.

Their actions
Flow from Grace
And this is
The sign of You
They carry.

The Not-Yet-Ripe
And the Ripe
Are both there
On the Earth.

Oh my soul,
Go and see it.

Understanding This Chapter

In the next four chapters, extremely fascinating advanced spiritual insights are shared. What is revealed is that your soul must climb five steps up a ladder to reach the final stage of maturity.

In this first chapter, you enter into a rarefied phase of spiritual discussion. Incorporating these new insights into your personal conduct will take you another step upward on the ladder to ending your karma.

First, please understand that by living a life of right action your soul mounts the first step to what's called the Plane of Righteousness, where you're inspired to learn about the Divine. In this first realm, your awareness of the laws of nature are enhanced: You understand that He made the world, with all its immutable laws, which cover everyone. No one, as I'm sure you know by now, can escape karma, the law of cause and effect—what you sow, you reap. You can end it, however, as you realize His Will for you and learn to live your dharma. When you live your dharma, you end your karma. Also, please recall that your absolute dharma is to always remember God.

Perhaps you've heard that everyone must have a life review before they die, even if they're killed suddenly, such as in an accident. Apparently, at this time your life flashes before your eyes and you're judged (most likely by yourself). I consider this to be the time of true heaven or hell. If you've lived a life of honor, you'll find inner peace at this juncture. To the contrary, if you've had less than a principled time on Earth, you're going to suffer during these final moments of existence.

What really brings you Divine peace and well-being at this critical instant is if you've developed unity with your Divine spiritual self. If you've focused on that aspect of living, you can close your eyes and go to your heavenly abode with no regrets, and grace in your heart.

Putting This Chapter to Work in Your Life

Affirm: *Today I will think, act, and speak for one purpose only. That purpose is to elevate everyone with whom I come in contact.*

My Reflections on This Chapter

_____

_____

_____

_____

_____

_____

_____

_____

❖ ❖ ❖

CHAPTER 36

So Many Things

*Understanding this chapter gives you the ability
to do your duty and fulfill your responsibility.*

In the Realm of Dharma,
Of Spiritual Law,
We come to understand
How to awaken ourselves
To ourselves.

In the Realm of Wisdom,
We speak
Of how everything
Gets accomplished.

There are so many
Winds, waters, and fires.

So many
Creative Forces.

So many
Creations
That the Creator
Is crafting,
Clothing the Spirit
In Form and Color.

So many actions
Done in so many
Lands and places,

So many places
That are not even
Known to us.

All for learning
What You want us
To learn.

So many Heavens,
Moons, and Suns.

So many Galaxies
With so many peoples.

So many joined
In Union with Thee.

So many wise ones
And masters.
So many
Robed goddesses.

So many gods
And demons.

So many persons of honor.

So many jewels of spiritual instruction
In so many Oceans of Existences.

So many ways
Of thinking about things.

So many words
That come from Thee.

So many rulers
Of Spiritual Nobility.

So many
Living attuned to Thee,
So many of Your servants.

Oh Seeker of Spirit,
Even Your limits
Are beyond limits.

Understanding This Chapter

Now the soul is rising to the Realm of Wisdom. Here you search for the truth, and in the process, you gain deep understanding and knowledge about the Infinite Creation and the workings of God. As a result of beginning to understand the incomprehensiveness of the workings of the Cosmos, your false sense of self, or ego, realizes its nothingness compared to your spirit.

If you take the time to read this chapter carefully, you'll feel the immense expansion of your soul's horizon. When this occurs, you'll relate to the diverse aspects of all created beings. You'll also clearly understand that we're all connected.

The two best emotions that describe this state of being are exhilaration and immense joy! Moreover, in this realm, you become aware of the many blessings that you have in your life.

Putting This Chapter to Work in Your Life

Affirm: *Today I will consider how my highest self has been revealed to me thus far. Was it all at once or in stages? Was it easy or difficult? Was it pleasant, uncomfortable, or perhaps both?*

My Reflections on This Chapter

_____

_____

_____

_____

_____

_____

_____

_____

❖ ❖ ❖

CHAPTER 37

Divine Realization

Knowing this chapter grants complete understanding
of the heavens and the earth.

In the Realm of Wisdom,
Wisdom is found.

There,
Beyond Sound,
The subtle
Vibratory frequency
Of creation
Creates the plays
And dramas.

In the Realm of Effort,
The Divine Word
Becomes form.

What is crafted there
Are creations
Of Incomparable Beauty.

It is impossible
To speak
Of these matters.

If someone
Tries to speak,
Afterwards,
He'll only feel mournful
That he couldn't
Describe it.

What is crafted there
Are persons of
Purity, clarity, and grace.
Attuned to the Divine
With minds
That know the difference
Between Truth and falsehood,
Persons of genuine understanding
And wisdom.

What is crafted there
Are the psyches
Of angels and masters.

Understanding This Chapter

Once you've entered the Realm of Wisdom, where you find truth and experience joy, living a material life may seem as if it's not very fulfilling. Those who continue to live primarily on the material plane without paying much attention to their spiritual development will be annoyed when small things go wrong. As time goes on and they age, a deep sense of emptiness begins to pervade their existence.

When allowed to endure, this sense of nothingness brings you an urgent and intense sense of longing for knowing the real spiritual self. Thereafter, they may begin to make an utmost effort to transform themselves by acting in accordance with their highest values. As a result of their striving, their awareness is profoundly refashioned to fully understand the delusion of *maya*, or the dream state of existence. As you know by now, it's this dream state that unfortunately tends to consume the life of so many "regular" people.

Once you have that understanding, you can see the insignificance of living a life guided by the emotional attachment of lower consciousness. The misery of living in such an inferior way may bring you intense displeasure, thus almost forcing you to surrender your will to that of your Higher Power. You now prefer to live attached only to the Divine.

After learning to dwell in the realm of your spirit, you experience ecstasy. Now life is at once enchantingly beautiful and yet sometimes rather mysterious. You are in awe of God.

It's possible that now you're attempting to listen for the still, small voice within yourself often, and you'll actually hear it frequently. You become enthralled by its power, and thus begin to get some insight into the majestic nature of the workings of the Universe. Your life becomes very satisfying as you begin to sense that you now lack nothing.

Putting This Chapter to Work in Your Life

Affirm: *Today I live in peace and harmony. I lovingly nurture my inner being.*

My Reflections on This Chapter

CHAPTER 38

Cutting Karma

Mastering this chapter eliminates the impact of all "bad" karma.

> In the Realm of Action,
> Your Sacred Words
> Are power,
>
> And there is no other power
> Besides it.
>
> In that Realm
> Are brave and strong
> Spiritual warriors
> Filled
> With the presence
> Of the Divine.

There,
It is a habit
Sewn securely
Inside them
To honor and praise
Thee.

These beautiful forms
Are impossible
To describe.

The Divine
Dwells
Within their minds.

There,
Those who have
Surrendered themselves
In love to Thee
Live as Lights.

They enjoy
Sweet-tasting bliss
Within themselves.

In the Realm of Truth,
The Formless One dwells.

By seeing All
That is continuously done,
The Divine looks kindly

Upon us and,
In that kind look,
Brings everything
To a state
Of completion.

There are worlds upon worlds,
Solar Systems,
Universes.

If someone tried
To describe them all,
There would be
No limit.

There,
Lights upon Lights
Come into bodies and forms.

And as the Divine Will
Guides them
So they act.

The Divine remains
In a state of contemplation
Seeing and enjoying it all.

Oh my soul,
Describing this
Forges the hard steel
Of Truth.

Understanding This Chapter

After being able to rise above the evanescent charms of the regular world, you climb the ladder to a level where you see how all of nature sits at the feet of God, relaxed and subjected to His Will.

His energy cleanses your soul and awakens its latent power. Your inner vision is no longer blinded by earthly matters. You become fully conscious of God and see Him everywhere. You come face-to-face with your own soul in its pure substance. You know yourself well, and are aware of your true origin. Now you're able to fully realize the God within your being.

This is the Realm of Action, and here you become totally imbued with the nectar of God's love. In a spiritual sense, you become immune to death, as you live merged in His light. You're now living free from delusion. After merging with the infinite while still a living, breathing human being (in other words, being "dead while alive") you're ceaselessly in bliss. This is the final stage of spiritual growth, the Realm of Truth.

But please do not ever forget that even after oneness is realized and you see that the Universe is functioning under His Will, your eyes can't see it all completely, your heart can feel only a minute drop of its awe, and your tongue can only just begin to describe your adoration.

Putting This Chapter to Work in Your Life

Affirm: *Today I will take the time to create my spiritual vision of surrender, compassion, and love. I will see how this vision shapes my reality and how my spiritual energy may create unity on Earth.*

My Reflections on This Chapter

_____

_____

_____

_____

_____

_____

_____

CHAPTER 39

Blessings

This chapter gives you the power to rewrite your own destiny.

Let the practice
Of restraining your desires
Be the furnace,

And let calmness
Be the goldsmith.

Let the mind
That knows the difference
Between Truth and falsehood
Be the anvil,

And let what you learn
From your own experience
Be the hammer.

Take your fear
And use it
To stoke the fires
Of your own spiritual discipline,

And let Love
Be the pot
In which the nectar
Of self-awakening,
Of self-awareness,
Is poured.

From that,
Fashion the coin
Of speaking
And living
Pure Truth.

Those upon whom
You look kindly,
Oh Divine Spirit,
Act in this way.

Oh my soul,
The Divine Gaze
Bestows a continuous grace
Which completes
Everything.

Understanding This Chapter

In this review chapter, the qualifications of successfully living a spiritual life are reviewed in a no-nonsense way. There are five in number:

1. **Chastity of word, thought, and deed.** This is the first prerequisite for the dawn of living a higher life and is the foundation of spirituality. As Jesus said, "Blessed are the pure in heart, for they shall see God." Purity is the key that unlocks the door of meditation leading to God. (Note that this isn't a reference to celibacy—it's a reference to honesty, honor, and purity in all behavior.)

2. **Patience** is the second spiritual attribute. It enables you to "go with the flow," thus bringing equilibrium and cheerfulness to your life.

3. You must have **control over your thoughts.** Remember the admonishment to "conquer your mind, and you'll conquer the world." By casting away your desires for ego gratification in favor of spiritual bliss, you'll enjoy great emotional equilibrium.

4. **Daily, steady spiritual practice and faith** will change your brain to function on a much higher level. Beyond that, it will also bring you better physical health, mental happiness, and emotional stability.

5. Finally, all spiritual seekers must gain the advantage of living in **devout awe of His presence.** We should all continually strive to achieve union with our Creator. And above all else, we need to love God with an intensity that burns up all our negativity and blazes the way to His door.

Putting This Chapter to Work in Your Life

Affirm: *Today I will meditate, concentrate, and contemplate the five attributes required to fullfill my goal of living a life of great spiritual fulfillment. I will take extra time to study the five characteristics of spiritual living and think about how I am doing.*

My Reflections on This Chapter

_____

_____

_____

_____

_____

_____

_____

CHAPTER 40

Divine Light

Completing this work brings self-satisfaction,
elevation, acknowledgement, and respect.

The Wind
Is the Guru,
The Teacher,
The Guide,

And Water
Is the Father.

The Mother
Is the great and honored
Earth.

Day and Night
Are the two nurses

In whose lap
The entire world
Plays.

All that is good,
All that is bad,
Are equally embraced
In the presence of the Divine
Under the command of Divine Law.

By your actions,
You, yourself, will know
How close you are to Truth
Or how far away.

Those
Who meditate
In the core
Of their being

Who earn themselves
Through their hard work—

Oh Nanak,
Their faces are radiant and beautiful
And so very many who are connected
With them
Are liberated, too.

Understanding This Chapter

In this finale, the complete summary of spirituality is related. You're given a view of life, its nature, its purpose, and its success and satisfaction. We're like children, nourished by our mother, Earth.

Every one of us sows the seeds of our actions and reaps the fruit of them. God's wisdom and judgment is immaculate. If you live in concert with your Higher Power, your behavior will bring you closer to God. If, for whatever reason (ignorance or foolishness, for example) you don't, you'll move further away from Him. It's actually that straightforward. In simple language, how you live your life on a daily basis determines your spiritual growth and grace. And of course, it's by His Will.

When you life a beautiful life of purity, consciousness, and love, you'll merge with the light of the Divine. And what's more, thanks to your good actions, your family will as well.

Because you discover and enjoy love, spiritual energy, and deep happiness in your life, when it's your time to leave your physical body to go to your heavenly abode, you'll have no regrets.

Putting This Chapter to Work in Your Life

1. Meditate upon where are you now spiritually compared to where you were before beginning this book.

2. After reading the next section, either return to the beginning and reread each chapter slowly, spending as many days as needed to grasp it before moving on to another, or pick one chapter and stay with it for 40 days.

My Reflections on This Chapter

_____

_____

_____

_____

_____

_____

_____

PART II

Two Meditations
to End Your Karma

A Brief History of Meditation

As you're most likely aware, the history of meditation stretches back for at least 5,000 years. And more than 1,500 years ago, Patanjali, a great Indian sage, composed a series of aphorisms, or *sutras,* to explain the art of yoga and meditation to his contemporaries. His words and ideas still live on today.

Patanjali believed that pure, eternal joy and peace are to be found only in union with our *Atman* or soul; that is, the God within. (Of course, uniting with your highest and best self is the benefit of reading and reflecting upon the 40 chapters in Part I of this book.) Patanjali also thought that attachment to the ego, or ignorance or the lower self, keeps us from that union.

Regardless of human beings' materialistic focus, the longing for happiness and the spiritual energy we call bliss remains. Unfortunately, without a regular spiritual practice, we're driven to seek our happiness in the false excitement of the external world. We become forced to accept substitutes for spirit and then persuade ourselves that the substitutes are genuine.

So it is only through a regular spiritual practice, including the reading of this book (and by the grace of God), that you can drop your lower obstacles to fulfilling your goal of spiritual bliss and find the inner peace that you seek.

Meditation's Journey to the West: A Brief Review

Throughout the 20th century, a few Indian yoga masters came to the West to share their sacred knowledge. It wasn't until 1948, however, that the foundation for understanding meditation from an occidental, academic perspective was laid. In that year, a Swiss-born physiologist named Walter Hess, Ph.D. brought the spotlight onto meditation when he won the famed Nobel Prize for demonstrating that there is an anti-stress spot in the brain. Hess showed that by stimulating a point in a cat's brain, specifically in one of the master control glands known as the *hypothalamus*, he could reproduce the stress response. When the point was activated, the animal's blood pressure would rise, and it would exhibit other telltale signs of stress, such as baring teeth. But when the probe was moved over slightly and then stimulated, the opposite response appeared: The cat became relaxed. Its blood pressure returned to normal, it relaxed its jaw, and it settled down. Hess then went on to prove that we humans have a natural anti-stress spot in our brain as well.

It took a couple of decades for the next great bit of experimental knowledge to be discovered. At that time, a young Harvard Medical School cardiologist named Herbert Benson, M.D., began studying the stress response. His work initially involved trying to raise and lower blood pressure in monkeys by using a set of flashing lights as a stimulus.

One day a young man named Robert Keith Wallace made an appointment to see Dr. Benson. He told the doctor that he and his friends could lower their own blood pressure at will by thinking a particular thought. Wallace, who held a Ph.D. in physiology, said that he practiced a technique called Transcendental Meditation (TM). The brazen young man then invited Dr. Benson to study him and his friends, rather than the monkeys.

As I've heard Dr. Benson say many times, "This was Harvard Medical School in 1968, so I asked him to leave."

Undeterred, Wallace returned again and again to try to convince Dr. Benson to do the research on TM. But the answer was always the same: "No, and there's the door."

Finally, Robert Keith Wallace convinced Dr. Benson to try a research study. Again, in Dr. Benson's words: "I told him to come at midnight and meet me at the back door. Then I took him down to the basement and hooked him up to my equipment."

Amazingly, the practitioners of meditation were able to do everything they said they could, and Dr. Benson was able to measure it all. This began a career-filling adventure for Dr. Benson, which continues as I write these words today.

In case you're not familiar with his work, Herbert Benson, M.D., didn't stop at studying TM. He believed that many other techniques could also lower stress—it was all part of the body's wisdom, and harkened back to the Nobel Prize–winning work of Dr. Walter Hess. Dr. Benson gave a name to the anti-stress effect. He called it the "relaxation response," and suggested that its many healthful and spiritual effects could be garnered if one were to practice it on a regular basis.

The regular elicitation of the relaxation response has been medically studied for many years now, and has been found to have numerous beneficial effects, including: a reduction in anxiety and blood pressure; an improvement in memory; less pain; increased fertility; and, astoundingly, a decrease in the incidence and severity of every illness studied. Meditation has been even been shown to help people reduce their cholesterol levels, rely on doctors and hospitals less, and live longer.

By far the most significant effect of meditation in regards to spiritual growth, however, is that when you meditate on a regular basis you gradually become aware of your Higher Power, God, the Universe, or whatever you want to call the Sacred Being in your life. Finding your spiritual essence in and of itself gives you more energy, improves your relationships with others, and allows you to be much more successful in your life.

The Fourth State

We all enter into three states of consciousness on a regular basis: the awake state, the sleep state, and the dream state. The fourth state, which is produced by meditation, prayer, or other spiritual practices, is transcendent and self-healing. It's here that you're able to discover your spiritual self.

There are four requirements to get into this state. Let's briefly take a look at each of them.

1. Comfort

Entering into the fourth state and discovering your soul doesn't require you to turn your legs into a pretzel—rather, you should be comfortable. You may sit on the floor with your legs crossed if you like, or you may relax in a comfortable chair. It's best not to lie down at this time because you may fall asleep. Recall that the sleep state is different from the spiritual state, so if you're sleepy, take a nap.

2. Quiet

When you meditate, the best results are usually achieved when you practice in a quiet environment, one that won't be interrupted by your landline or cell phone, your children, or your pets. This is your time to carve out some peace, and it needs to be as silent as possible. If your spouse, partner, friend, or significant other is joining you, that's great; if not, don't forget that this time is *for yourself.*

3. A Tool

If you were to put a nail into a wall, you'd need a tool, such as a hammer. To meditate you need the same thing. In basic techniques such as the relaxation response, TM, or mindfulness, that tool can be any thought, sound, short prayer, or phrase upon which you choose to concentrate. You may also focus on your breathing.

Sample words often used are *one, om, Sat Nam, peace, love,* or a short prayer from your own faith ("Jesus loves me,"

"Our Father, who art in heaven," or Shalom, for example). The chosen word should be a positive one, so *divorce* or *alimony* is not the best choice for a meditative word. I'll share the complete technique with you in a moment.

4. An Attitude

This is the most important ingredient in the recipe of meditation. As you enter into the fourth state, you'll notice that your mind is bombarded by thoughts. Many people become discouraged by these thoughts—please don't be one of them.

The reason people become disheartened is because they think that they aren't "good" at meditation. "After all," they figure, "I should be able to just 'blank out my mind.'" Not true! The release of energy in the form of these thoughts is the mechanism by which you rejuvenate and regenerate your body, mind, and spirit during meditation. It's the process by which you gain insight into your true nature.

I've personally been meditating for more than a quarter of a century, and I still have tons of thoughts almost every time I meditate. They may go something like this: *I wish I'd gone to the bathroom first. . . . When is my father-in-law going back to Italy? . . . I wonder if I should refinance the mortgage. . . . Where the heck is Bob? He was supposed to be here an hour ago. . . . I wonder what happened to Joan from the first grade. . . .* and so on.

Sound familiar? When your mind begins to wander away from your tool or mantra, you simply start all over again. What I mean is that when other thoughts enter your mind, you need to go back and favor your breath, word, thought, or whatever. You begin again by returning to your tool. If your mantra is the word *one,* for example, and your name is Nancy, you can favor your tool by inhaling your breath and saying something to yourself like, "Oh, well, Nancy, relax. . . . One."

The Next Level

It's possible that you may be a beginner in meditation or a newcomer to spirituality—but my feeling is that if you're reading this book, you've probably been a spiritual seeker for some time and are ready to move beyond the basics. As you know, the 40 verses of Guru Nanak's Japji Sahib that you've read and hopefully studied will change your consciousness by themselves. Those words have magical power, and reading and contemplating them will deliver you to your soul and the God within yourself. But in addition to these 40 chapters, I'd like to offer you some "dessert." Some icing on the cake, shall we say?

I'd now like to present you with two beautiful meditations that will take you to the next level of your spiritual growth in concert with reading the 40 chapters. The two parts of this book fit together like a hand and a beautiful, soft glove.

Before I actually share the meditations with you, however, please allow me to continue with a brief description of a more advanced approach to meditation, because having this knowledge will make it easier for you to understand how to do them.

In addition to using the four steps described on pages 221 to 222, the next level of meditation also asks you to focus on some specific techniques. Let's examine each one in brief.

1. Breathwork

In the two meditations presented here, your breathing will be simple. In the first one, the breath will be allowed to flow naturally; in the second, the pattern will be one long deep breath per repetition of the mantra.

2. Posture

The position will also be easy. You will simply sit up straight in a comfortable cross-legged posture on the floor or, alternatively, you may sit in a chair.

3. Mantras

You will be using two different sounds or mantras. Why? Well, as I previously wrote in my book *Meditation as Medicine,* different sounds have different effects because they stimulate the 84 acupuncture meridian points on the upper palate of your mouth in a unique way. The vibration at the point of contact of the tongue with the points on the upper palate sends a particular energy up to the pituitary gland, which is located exactly on the other side of the top of your mouth. These vibrations and energy act as signals, causing your pituitary to orchestrate the release of healing chemicals. The chemicals thereafter course throughout your body and mind, delivering a message of peace, tranquility, and bliss. And as I'll explain in a bit more detail in a moment, these advanced meditations change the activity of your brain from everyday thinking to that of spiritual thought.

The word *mantra* can be broken down into two different parts: *man,* which means "human being," and *tra,* which means "tool." So a mantra, therefore, is simply a tool for a human being to get a desired consequence. (When I discuss the second meditation, I'll have more to say about the specificity of certain mantras.)

4. Mudra

Differing *mudras,* or hand positions, are also utilized to create different effects, depending on the meditation's desired outcome. Mudras work because the hands and fingers are very highly represented in the brain. Consequently, the use of finger touching (so effective in brain-injury recovery, for example), is quite beneficial in activating different anatomical parts of the brain, which gives different effects.

5. Focus of Concentration

Not unlike basic meditation, the more sophisticated variety you're about to encounter require a specific focus of concentration. Only now, your attention will be directed toward more than just engaging the sound. As you'll soon see in the first mind/body meditation exercise, the focus can come in the form of visualization.

Spiritual Bliss in Only 12 Minutes a Day

Imagine being able to activate your "God gene" and stimulate the spiritual spot in your brain in just a few minutes a day. Although many gifted spiritual teachers and mind/body therapists recommend meditating for 20 to 30 minutes at a time to realize the spiritual benefits of meditation, my recent research using sophisticated brain x-rays (called SPECT scans), reveals that you can reach a state of heightened awareness, relaxation, and bliss in only *12* minutes.

Previous research done at the University of Pennsylvania (which was also featured in magazines such as *Time* and *Newsweek*) disclosed that it took the subjects in this meditation research about an hour to obtain feelings of spirituality. In those studies, it was seen that the deeper these people descended into meditation or prayer, the more active their frontal lobes and limbic system became. The frontal-lobe stimulation implied better ability to focus and concentrate, while the limbic system being activated is thought to turn on spiritual feelings such as rapture and ecstasy in the meditator.

Equally revealing is the fact that at the same time these regions flash to life, another important region—the parietal lobe near the back of the brain—goes dim. This lobe orients a person to time and space. In other words, when you meditate, you create the feeling of having God close at hand and of being at one with the Universe. When you combine everything that goes on in your brain while reading a chapter each day (which also produces spiritual changes in your consciousness), followed by the meditation exercises, the result is profound and spiritual. Now you can have this experience faster by practicing either or both of the two following meditations for only 12 minutes a day each.

Because it's so important, let me summarize the results of this research again: Previous studies disclosed that it took subjects one hour to "be there," but *my research cut the time down to 12 minutes.*

It's when you have the spiritual experiences such as those produced in this research on a regular basis that you come to live in what's called "higher consciousness." This is dharma . . . and please recall that when you live your dharma, that's when you end your karma. The meditations in this book end your karma because they help you feel God in your soul *every time* you practice them. Moreover, combining these two meditations with the chapter of the day helps you make progress rapidly in your search for your spirit because, as you recall, these meditations work fast.

As you practice these sacred meditations with devotion, you will connect to your higher self. You'll burn through your past karma, as well as bringing balance and total prosperity to your life. And when you discover your true spiritual self, you live the essence of dharma. That takes you beyond karma to the ecstasy of bliss.

There are 30 trillion cells of light in you, and within each cell lives God. That means you have 30 trillion dancing, living Gods inside your being.

Let's wake them up.

Bring Total Balance to Your Life with Kirtan Kriya

The first meditation is called *Kirtan Kriya,* or the "five primal sounds" meditation. As you may recall from reading Chapter 20, primal sounds are what you hear when you listen for the Word of God within your being, and what you feel when you tune in to His Will. Primal sounds are the essence, or the Nam, of the Creator and the focus of spiritual living. This meditative mind/body exercise uses the five primal sounds of the Universe to produce its wondrous benefits. It celebrates the cycle of creation: birth, life, death, and infinity. It also activates and balances your five elements, which I'll explain in detail momentarily.

As you may know, *Kirtan* means "singing," while *Kriya* means "a spiritual exercise complete in itself." Therefore, the Kirtan Kriya is a singing meditation whose many benefits make it complete in itself. If I were stranded on a desert island and was allowed only one meditation, this is the one I'd pick. As the master of kundalini yoga and meditation, Yogi Bhajan, once said, "All meditation begins and ends with Kirtan Kriya."

This exercise is so powerful because it brings you the gift of totally balancing your personality—it also helps you live your *life* in balance. I've known many people who have enjoyed this outcome after practicing Kirtan Kriya. It brings this balance because, according to Eastern medicine, it equalizes all of the five elements: fire, earth, air, water, and wood. Each one of these elements carries with it a personality trait or characteristic and may also correspond to a particular organ system and illness in the body. For example:

— Element number one, **fire**, represents an exploding type of anger in a type A personality trait. The fire element also relates to your heart and cardiovascular system: When it's out of balance, your blood pressure rises, you feel tense, and you can eventually develop heart disease severe enough to cause a heart attack. From a spiritual perspective, it's virtually impossible to be openhearted or compassionate when this element is out of balance, because you're so constricted.

— The second element, **earth**, signifies the trait of contemplation or, when out of balance, obsession. When balanced, the earth element adds sweetness and "earthiness" to your personality. In other words, you're "down to earth." This is important when you're on a spiritual path because you need to have your feet firmly on the ground and live as part of the world, rather than walking around with your head in the clouds.

Organs that can be affected negatively when this element is out of order include the entire gastrointestinal system, especially your stomach. When your stomach is amiss, you'll notice it because your digestion will be off and you may have too much acid, resulting in heartburn. Many people are out of balance in this area, as evidenced by all the television ads for one type of acid reducer or another, or a particular stomach-coating product.

— One of the most beautiful things about Kirtan Kriya is that it helps heal depression by balancing the third element of **air.** If you have the feeling of not being nurtured enough as a child, or of not being taken care of or supported as an adult, chances are that your air element is out of balance. This doesn't mean that your perception is incorrect; you may very well have been abused. Many people in my medical practice have this idea, and it's usually correct on one level or another.

Regardless of the cause or perception of it, this element is still out of whack when you're depressed. When a person has lost the ability to elevate him- or herself, that is precisely the root cause of depression. Kirtan Kriya restores your ability to elevate and balance yourself. And most remarkably, it works the very first time.

From a physical standpoint, air is associated with lung energy. So if it's out of balance, you may have an oppressive feeling of shortness of breath. You may also have medical conditions such as asthma or other forms of chronic lung disease or respiratory allergies. An imbalance in your air element, being depressed, feeling a lack of nurturing, and developing lung problems often go together. (In a moment I'll discuss how having an imbalance in your lung energy or element can also lead to anger, which in and of itself is horribly damaging to your health.)

— The fourth element, **water,** is significant because when in proper balance, it's the seat of spiritual realization. When this element is off, however, people will act insolent, as if they have a chip on their shoulder—they're not very attractive to be around. They're often easily irritated and can make you feel like you're trying to breathe underwater, as if you're trapped. You simply can't wait to get away from this type of person because they're like psychic vampires who drain you of energy. Additionally, from a physical standpoint, when someone's fourth element or water element is off, he or she may develop kidney or bladder problems, including infections, stones, or cancerous tumors.

When the water element is restored to order and in proper balance, the word to describe this person is *charismatic;* after all, one who is spiritually realized certainly has a nice glow to his or her countenance.

— Finally, we come to the fifth element, or **wood.** Balance here is crucial to being healthy, happy, and content with life because when it's affected negatively, you'll be suffering miserably. You see, when the wood element is out of balance, you'll have difficulty resolving conflicts and forgiving anyone, especially yourself. Actually, *you're* the most important person you need to forgive and be compassionate toward. Without loving yourself enough to release your self-animosity, you won't be able to forgive anyone else either. This is a very unpleasant way to live. For the reason alone of bringing peace to your life, it's worthwhile to practice Kirtan Kriya on a regular basis.

A person who's angry and can't forgive walks around in a lot of pain. Unresolved conflicts create such a sorry state of affairs inside your body that your cells secrete all kinds of harmful chemicals, which some prominent doctors believe may lead to an immune-compromised state. This can allow cancer to develop inside of the body, with all its difficult and painful life-changing occurrences. If a person has cancer or another life-threatening illness, then resolving conflicts and forgiving others is a vitally important part of the healing process.

A moment ago, I alluded to the fact that being out of balance in the wood element may lend itself to chronic anger. Here's how that happens: Usually the air element has the responsibility of keeping the wood element in check, but when air is out of balance (such as when a person is depressed), this check-and-balance system doesn't occur. Consequently, wood is allowed to rage out of control, and the person may then suffer from uncontrollable anger.

Perhaps you've seen this in action. If you've ever known someone who was depressed, for example, recall that when they weren't blue they were probably angry. In other words, they'd "flip-flop" back and forth between anger and depression. That isn't a fun way to live—and it doesn't lend itself to spiritual advancement either, at least not while the person is suffering from their depression. But when the depression clears and the person has rediscovered the way to elevate his- or herself by practicing Kirtan Kriya and taking care in other ways, the terrible pain suffered during the depression can act as a catalyst toward creating new heights of spiritual growth.

An imbalance in the wood element is made a lot worse over time if you don't work to resolve your conflicts with others and practice forgiveness for past wrongs done against you—both real and imagined. Family dynamics are a challenge sometimes, yet it's crucial for everyone's peace of mind to do whatever is possible to keep the energy clear. Go that extra mile and make the necessary effort to resolve conflicts and dissolve anger and resentment.

Chanting the five primal sounds found in Kirtan Kriya (which are described below) will balance your energy, clear your consciousness, and help you forgive yourself and others.

It's a marvelous way to discover the majesty of your mystical self. And it only takes 12 minutes a day!

Kirtan Kriya: The "Five Primal Sounds" Meditation to End Your Karma

Do you remember the four ingredients necessary to enter into the fourth state created by basic meditation? They are comfort, quiet, a tool, and a special attitude. The mind/body exercise I'm about to share with you utilizes those same four steps, but it doesn't stop there. It also employs the five additional ingredients I mentioned to give it immense power, precision, and practicality.

The five new parts, in addition to the four original aspects of basic meditation, as you recall, are breath, posture, healing sounds, hand position, and a unique focus of concentration. (The figures shown depict how to do the meditation.)

1. Breath

The breath comes naturally—you won't even have to think about it. All you have to do is inhale to begin and then follow the instructions below (you can also follow the CD I mention on page 247).

2. Posture

You can sit comfortably in a chair or cross-legged on the floor, in what we call "easy pose." There is no difference in the result, as long as you sit up fairly straight.

3. Sound

We utilize the five primal sounds: *Sa, Ta, Na,* and *Ma,* because they're the five most healing sounds in the Universe. You might say, "But those are only four sounds." That's correct, but the *ahh* at the end of each primal sound is common to all of them; thus, it is the fifth sound. In essence, it looks more like this: *Saa, Taa, Naa,* and *Maa.*

4. Hand Position

As you can see, when you chant the sound *Sa,* you touch your thumb to your index finger. When you say *Ta,* you touch your thumb to your middle finger. With *Na,* you touch your thumb to your ring finger. Finally, with *Ma,* your thumb and pinky touch.

5. Focus of Concentration

You can see by the diagram on the next page that the L form of meditation is used as a focal point in Kirtan Kriya. As you chant each sound, imagine it entering the top of your head and leaving through the middle of your forehead in a sweeping L motion. The movement is like that of a broom.

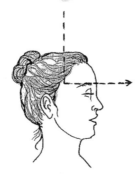

From an energetic perspective, the sound is opening the channel between the seventh energy center of your body, which corresponds to your pineal gland, with the one corresponding with your pituitary gland, or the sixth energy center. This helps you develop tremendous intuition, which aids in ending your karma. As a matter of fact, it's written in the original description of this meditation that one who does it on a regular basis will "know the unknown and see the unseen."

6. Time

This meditation is done for 12 minutes in the following manner: Chant it out loud for 2 minutes, then in a stage whisper for 2 minutes, then silently for 4 minutes, followed by 2 minutes in a whisper, and wrapping up with 2 minutes out loud. Make sure that you continue to touch your fingers, even during the silent part.

To end the meditation, inhale deeply through your nose, hold your breath for a moment, and then exhale through your nose. Repeat this process twice more and then relax.

End Your Karma and Connect with the Endless Circle of Infinite Prosperity

As you recall from the Introduction, an entire oak tree resides in a tiny acorn. All that has to happen is for Mother Nature or take over—when she does, everything that the acorn needs to become a giant oak tree is drawn to it: water, rain, sun, minerals from the soil, and so on.

It can be the same in your life: You can draw exactly what you need to be as healthy, happy, and successful as you desire. You have the capacity to direct your mind and send out the energy that will draw everything you need back to you.

Technically speaking, you have to have some time and discipline for tuning in to the Universe and the energy that can have a positive effect in your life. You actually need to project out your intention with a force adequate enough to hook up with the exact energetic vibration that you need. That's why I suggested in the Introduction and elsewhere that's it best to arise and read the book and meditate in the ambrosial early hours of the day. This is the time to connect with your true identity, and it's the best time to count your blessings! This action alone will go a long way to ending your karma.

You must find time for yourself, your identity, your values, your virtues, and your deepest thoughts. Only within yourself can you find your true identity—nobody else can find it for you. You must rise in the morning and find your true self. You need this time to be all to yourself, where there is virtually no one else. It will bring you prosperity.

Every element of the Universe is in a constant state of vibration, which is then manifested to us as light, sound, and energy. You can tune your own highest consciousness into the awareness of that totality with the use of a mantra. When you vibrate in rhythm with your breath to a particular sound current, you can expand your sensitivity to the entire spectrum of sound vibrations and, just like the acorn, you will attract exactly what you need to fulfill your destiny. It's similar to a note on a stringed instrument. In other words, as you vibrate, the entire Universe vibrates with you. This is the true meaning of prosperity.

Mantras and Ending Your Karma

As Yogi Bhajan once said, "Mantras are not small things. They are mind vibrations in relationship to the Cosmos. The science of mantra is based on the knowledge that sound is a form of energy having structure, power, and a definite predictable effect on the chakras and the human psyche. Each time you perfect a mantra, you are like a master musician who can evoke elevated states of being from the instrument of self."

So just as a mantra is the mind's relationship to the Cosmos, every single word you say is a confirmation of that relationship. The words you use in your everyday life, for example, reinforce again and again the structure of the physical, emotional, and financial reality in which you live—whether you're happy, depressed, prosperous, broke, or successful. Your inner mantras, or the dialogue you repeat to yourself on a regular basis, can bring you the grace of your Divinity, your dharma, or even your karma.

Taking that into consideration, three mantras you should never say because of the potential negative effect that they have on you are *I don't know, I'm not ready,* or *I can't do it.*

Harnessing the power of mantra can be a useful tool to bring about positive change in your consciousness and your life. Again, according to Yogi Bhajan, "It is a fact: You may not deserve something, and there may not be the situation for it, but God, you will have it. In this case it's not your karma that matters; it's the mantra that matters.

"After all," he continued, "in the beginning there was sound; there was the word; the word was with God, and the word was God. That created the Universe, it manifested the Universe."

The Mantra to End Your Karma and Connect with the Endless Circle of Infinite Prosperity

As you now know and appreciate, mantras are formulas that alter the patterns of the mind and the chemistry of the brain. Chanting mantras, either silently or aloud, is a totally conscious method of controlling and directing your mind. And as I've just described, it's a very precise way to attract what you desire and need in your life. Happiness, sorrow, joy, and regret are vibratory frequencies of the mind; some people may call them attitudes or beliefs, but they are fundamentally vibratory frequencies or thought waves. These mantras determine the kind of program played by your mind.

The vibration you create becomes your scenario, as it defines how you feel and what you project to others. You exercise your right to choose at any time. You are creating your destiny with every word you speak: Whether it's for prosperity, peace of mind, increasing intuition, or any of the other multitude of possible benefits inherent in mantras, simply by chanting them you'll be setting vibrations into motion that will have a profound effect on your life.

This second meditation is technically very easy, but the mantra used in it is incredibly potent. That's why I've spent this time preparing you to understand the power of mantras. This particular one attracts to you all of the incredible prosperity power of the Universe. It's much more impressive to practice and experience it than discuss it, so here is how it's done.

1. Breath

Take one long, deep breath in through the nose. Try to use this one breath to sing the entire mantra. If, for any reason, you run out of air, rather than taking in another deep breath, simply sniff in a little air through your nose.

2. Posture

Sit in a comfortable cross-legged posture on the floor or normally in a chair. Keep your back straight.

3. Sound

The mantra is: *Hari, Hari, Hari, Hari, Hari, Hari, Har.*

The last word, *Har,* is held out the same length of time that it takes to chant the first six *Haris.* (Note that "Hari" doesn't sound like "Harry"—it's the same as in Hari Krishna, although there's no relationship between the two.) It takes the same amount of time (approximately 10 seconds) to sing the first six *Hari,* as it takes to chant the final *Har.* Therefore, the entire repetition of the mantra takes a total of around 20 seconds.

The mantra is chanted in a monotone, with the *Har* in a lower pitch at the end of the chant. After a few repetitions, you'll tune in to your tone that is in harmony with the Universe. Everyone has a natural pitch that harmonizes with the Universal Pitch. You'll find a sound current that feels comfortable to you, and that vibration will open you up to your Higher Power and put you in harmony with the Universe. (Please refer to page 247 to read about my CD or DVD. I think you'll not only find it easier to use either or both of them, but you'll also enjoy the musical accompaniment.)

4. Hand Position

Put your left hand, palm facing up, at the level of your diaphragm; then put your right hand on top of your left hand with the fingers straight and your palm facing up. Touch your thumbs together lightly.

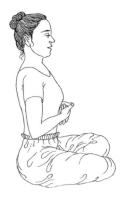

5. Focus of Concentration

Concentrate on the sound, and really engage the mantra. Focus your attention on the spot between your eyebrows at the root or top of your nose. This is known as the "third eye" point, and it's almost right between your eyebrows. This action will accentuate your intuition and help draw to you exactly what you need.

I suggest that you don't put too much energy into the form your prosperity will take, because the reality is that the Universe will bring you exactly what you need. Sometimes it's more than you'd expect or want, and sometimes it's totally different from what you desire. So just relax into the meditation and enjoy it. Attune yourself to the energy of the Cosmos, and allow yourself to manifest what God has in store for you.

In my experience, you'll receive everything you need by doing this meditation, so it's important to place yourself into a receptive mode, as opposed to pursuing it aggressively. *Let the Universe serve you.*

This meditation opens you up to attracting and receiving exactly what you need, so let the law of attraction work for you. You may want to consider cultivating the idea that you don't simply desire to end your karma or attract prosperity into your life; rather, you actually deserve it. In other words, deserve, don't desire.

The meditation can effectively be done for 11 minutes to start. After you learn how to do it properly and increase your ability and endurance, you can practice it for 31 minutes. To end the meditation after the 11 or 31 minutes of practice, inhale through your nose, hold your breath for 5 to 10 seconds, and then exhale through your nose. Repeat this process two more times.

As you inhale the first time, feel that you are totally complete. You already have everything you need—you simply have to accept it. As you exhale, feel this energy permeate every cell in your body. The second time, you can inhale knowledge, wisdom, and healing. As you exhale, release all your pain, anxiety, stress, and suffering back to the Universe. As you inhale the final time, tighten the base of your spine and pull all of your energy up. As you exhale your breath out this last time, deeply relax.

Afterword

Keeping Up

Well, you've done it. You've taken a quantum leap toward ending your karma, living your dharma, and remembering God with every breath. Beyond that, by practicing the two prized meditations presented in Part II, you're bringing balance into your life, as well as attracting to you now all of the beautiful aspects of total prosperity that the Universe has in store for you. What a magnificent accomplishment—congratulations!

I'm very grateful that we could spend this time together, for I feel purified myself from writing this book and having you read it. Thank you for joining me on this wonderful journey to the center of your soul. Perfect peace, tranquility, and joy are certainly here.

But there's one more thing I'd like you to consider. And that's . . . what's next? If you've read and reflected upon the 40 chapters herein, and perhaps begun to feel their power, what should you do now? The answer is clear: Keep up! I mean keep your spiritual energy up. For example, I suggest that you keep your morning practice going, start every day in a positive way, and continue to take care of yourself. Don't stop now that you're making such tremendous progress!

Once a bright student asked the master an important question. "Sir," she said, "you're a master. Why do you still get up early every morning to read Japji and meditate?"

"Because I want to stay a master," he said vibrantly with a glowing smile.

Yes, it's true that you've made enormous strides and ended your karma. But now is the time to keep up and keep going. Here's how you can continue to take quantum leaps in your spiritual growth and continue to progress on the never-ending path of Divine well-being:

1. Wake up early every morning, breathe deeply, and reread one of your favorite chapters of the book. Then "seal it" and lock in its effects with one of the meditations.

2. Another (perhaps more effective and valuable) way to proceed is to pick one chapter and reread and study it every day for 40 days. As I'm sure you're aware, 40 is a highly spiritual number—for example, Jesus fasted in the desert for 40 days before he received his ultimate blessing of enlightenment. You can then also practice the meditation of your choice daily after rereading that chapter.

3. You can also read a different chapter every day and then take one of the meditations and keep up with it specifically for 40 days (after all, it takes that long to master a meditation).

At the end of that time, you'll be sure to have drawn its benefits to you: be it balance, grace, or prosperity.

4. Perhaps the most powerful way to proceed is to pick one chapter and study it for 40 days, followed by the same meditation every day for 40 days, too. A very effective way is to begin at Chapter 1 and go in order. You can combine that with alternating the meditations, doing one and then the other for 40 days each. At the end of doing this practice, you'll find the treasure that is the birthright of every human: infinite unconditional happiness.

Whichever method you choose, you'll certainly keep up with ending your karma and living your dharma. You'll be so in tune with your best self that there will be no difference between you and God.

I'd like to send you on your way now with all my best wishes, love, and blessings.

In the name of the Cosmos, which prevails through everybody, and the holy Nam, which holds the world, I wish you perfect peace, tranquility, and joy.

May the longtime sun shine upon you.

All love surround you.

And the pure light within you

Guide your way on, and on, and on . . .

Sat Nam.

Inhale deeply. Hold your breath. Exhale and relax.

Peace to all, life to all, love to all.

About the Author

Dharma Singh Khalsa, M.D., often referred to simply as "Dr. Dharma," was born in Ohio and raised in Florida. An anesthesiologist by training, he's a true leader and pioneer in the field of integrative medicine. As the President/Medical Director of the Alzheimer's Prevention Foundation International in Tucson, Arizona, Dr. Dharma was the first physician to testify before the Congress of the United States about his innovative ideas on the prevention and treatment of Alzheimer's disease.

An ordained minister and yogi, Dr. Dharma is the author of the critically acclaimed, best-selling books *The New Golden Rules, Brain Longevity, The Pain Cure, Meditation as Medicine,* and *Food as Medicine.* He's also the developer of the first-ever kit to improve brain power: *The Better Memory Kit.*

Dr. Dharma has also produced a meditation CD series and pop-music album entitled *Love Is In You,* featuring his group, *Bliss.* He lives in Tucson, Arizona, with his wife, Kirti, who's originally from Rome, Italy. He lectures and consults worldwide.

To learn more about Dr. Dharma's work, including scheduling a memory-loss reversal or spirituality consultation, please visit his Website: **www.drdharma.com**, or contact him at:

Dharma Singh Khalsa, M.D.
2420 N. Pantano Road
Tucson, AZ 845715
Phone: (520) 749-8374
Fax: (520) 296-6640

At **www.drdharma.com**, you'll also find his free newsletter, *The Healing Zone,* which has tips on living a healthier, happier, longer, and more spiritual life. Topics include how to meditate more effectively, how to lose weight safely, which vitamins and memory-specific nutrients help reverse memory loss, how to have more energy, how to communicate better, and how to be more successful.

Also, log on (or to **www.hayhouseradio.com**) to enjoy Dr. Dharma's Internet radio show, also called *The Healing Zone,* every Wednesday at 2 P.M. Pacific Standard Time. He has great guests and discusses up-to-the-minute health information you won't find anywhere else.

CDs, DVDs, and videos of the two meditation exercises in this book (and in Dr. Dharma's other books) are also available on **www.drdharma.com**.

Acknowledgments

The lovely words of Guru Nanak's Japji are brought to life in *The End of Karma* thanks to the excellent translation by Ek Ong Kaar Kaur Khalsa, author of *The Song of the Soul*. It's with her kind permission that this translation of Guru Nanak's original work is used in this book.

I am eternally grateful to my teacher, His Holiness Siri Singh Sahib, Yogi Bhajan (1926–2004), who inspired me to live to my highest consciousness.

I also wish to thank my good friend and colleague Livtar Singh Khalsa, affectionately known as Master L., for his help with the meditations, especially the musical renditions of them (which you can find on page 247).

I'd like to thank Martine Rothblatt, J.D., Ph.D, and her partner, Bina, for their friendship and support.

My heartfelt love and gratitude go to my lovely wife, Kirti Kaur Khalsa, who is my greatest supporter. Kirti skillfully read and edited the manuscript; served as a sounding board for my ideas; and, as always, helped me get the book done on time and in good shape. I cannot overestimate her contribution, nor can I thank her enough for all her help.

Thanks also to Siri Kartar Kaur Khalsa for her work on the illustrations.

And last, but certainly not least, I offer my appreciation to my fantastic office staff: Martin, Peggy, and Kelly. Thanks for all your help.

Hay House Titles of Related Interest

Ask and It Is Given: *Learning to Manifest Your Desires,*
by Esther and Jerry Hicks (The Teachings of Abraham)

A Deep Breath of Life: *Daily Inspiration for
Heart-Centered Living,* by Alan Cohen

The Disappearance of the Universe: *Straight Talk
about Illusions, Past Lives, Religion, Sex, Politics, and
the Miracles of Forgiveness,* by Gary R. Renard

Everything I've Ever Done That Worked, by Lesley Garner

The Gift of Peace: *Guideposts on the
Road to Serenity,* by Ben Stein

**Mending the Past and Healing the Future with Soul
Retrieval,** by Alberto Villoldo, Ph.D.

The Power of Intention: *Learning to Co-create Your World
Your Way,* by Dr. Wayne W. Dyer

Power vs. Force: *The Hidden Determinants of Human Behavior,*
by David Hawkins, M.D., Ph.D.

You Can Heal Your Life, by Louise L. Hay

All of the above are available at your local
bookstore, or may be ordered by visiting:
Hay House USA: **www.hayhouse.com;** Hay House
Australia: **www.hayhouse.com.au;** Hay House UK:
www.hayhouse.co.uk; Hay House South Africa:
orders@psdprom.co.za

We hope you enjoyed this Hay House book.
If you'd like to receive a free catalog featuring additional
Hay House books and products, or if you'd like information about
the Hay Foundation, please contact:

Hay House, Inc.
P.O. Box 5100
Carlsbad, CA 92018-5100

(760) 431-7695 or **(800) 654-5126**
(760) 431-6948 (fax) or **(800) 650-5115 (fax)**
www.hayhouse.com

❖❖

Published and distributed in Australia by:
Hay House Australia Pty. Ltd. • 18/36 Ralph St.
Alexandria NSW 2015 • *Phone:* 612-9669-4299
Fax: 612-9669-4144 • www.hayhouse.com.au

Published and distributed in the United Kingdom by:
Hay House UK, Ltd. • Unit 62, Canalot Studios
222 Kensal Rd., London W10 5BN • *Phone:* 44-20-8962-1230
Fax: 44-20-8962-1239 • www.hayhouse.co.uk

Published and distributed in the Republic of South Africa by:
Hay House SA (Pty), Ltd., P.O. Box 990, Witkoppen 2068
Phone/Fax: 27-11-706-6612 • orders@psdprom.co.za

Distributed in Canada by: Raincoast
9050 Shaughnessy St., Vancouver, B.C. V6P 6E5
Phone: (604) 323-7100 • *Fax:* (604) 323-2600

❖❖

Tune in to **www.hayhouseradio.com**™ for the best in
inspirational talk radio featuring top Hay House authors! And,
sign up via the Hay House USA Website to receive the Hay House
online newsletter and stay informed about what's going on with
your favorite authors. You'll receive bimonthly announcements
about: Discounts and Offers, Special Events, Product Highlights,
Free Excerpts, Giveaways, and more!
www.hayhouse.com